THE NAMES OF GOD

Fini
6 aug 2011
I expected more
meat, but got a
lot of fluff.

LESTER SUMRALL

THE
NAMES
OF
GOD

WHITAKER
HOUSE

THE NAMES OF GOD
updated edition

ISBN-13: 978-0-88368-779-6
ISBN-10: 0-88368-779-8
Printed in the United States of America
© 1982 by Lester Sumrall Evangelistic Association (LeSEA)

1030 Hunt Valley Circle
New Kensington, PA 15068
www.whitakerhouse.com

Library of Congress Catalog-in-Publication Data
Sumrall, Lester Frank, 1913–1996.
The names of God / Lester Sumrall.—Updated ed.
p.   cm.
Summary: "Explores the characteristics of God as revealed through His biblical names"—Provided by publisher.
ISBN-13: 978-0-88368-779-6 (trade pbk. : alk. paper)
ISBN-10: 0-88368-779-8 (trade pbk. : alk. paper)
1. God—Names—Sermons. 2. Sermons, American—20th century. I. Title.
BT180.N2S95 2006
231—dc22
2006015719

6 7 8 9 10 11 12 13 14 15 16 ⨆⨆ 16 15 14 13 12 11 10 09 08 07

CONTENTS

CHAPTER 1

WHAT'S IN A NAME?

The great poet William Shakespeare once posed this question:

> What's in a name? That which we call a rose
> By any other name would smell as sweet.

And most people today would agree. Our modern society places little significance on the meaning of a name. Parents usually name their children after beloved relatives or well-known persons. Sometimes they pick a child's name merely because it "sounds good." But seldom would they give any thought to the meaning of a name.

Yet names do mean something. Ideally, they correspond directly to the one designated by the name. For example, did you know that the name *Kenneth* comes from the Greek word meaning "to know"? So a person named Kenneth is supposed to be knowledgeable. Since the name *Diana* comes from the Greek word meaning "of a god," a girl with that name is supposed to be "simply divine" in her beauty or other qualities. Other people's names are derived from words of the ancient Greek, Latin, Norse, or other languages. And most of those names have some special meaning.

The same is true of place names. You probably know, for example, that the name *Philadelphia* means "city of brotherly love." It comes from the Greek words *phileo* ("to love") and *delphos* ("city"). The name *Jerusalem* means "city of peace," being derived from the Hebrew word *shalom* ("peace"). There is probably some significance behind the name of your town or city.

My point is simply this: While it may have been all right for Shakespeare to shrug off the importance of a name, we should not take names so lightly. Often a name provides an important clue to the nature of a person or place.

This is certainly true of God. The Bible refers to God by many different names, and each one reveals some aspect of God's character or His relationship with us. The translators who gave us the King James Version and other English versions of the Bible simply translate His name as "God" or "LORD"; but significantly, several Greek or Hebrew names are used in the original manuscripts. If you want to become a serious student of the Word of God, you should be familiar with those Greek and Hebrew names because they contain a wealth of truth about the wonderful God we serve.

GOD'S CREDENTIALS

For centuries, people did not know the name of God. That may come as a surprise to you, but it's true. When God walked with Adam and Eve in the garden of Eden, it wasn't necessary for them to know His name because they knew Him intimately. They did not need to call upon Him or invoke Him in prayer for He was their daily companion. Then they disobeyed Him and were driven out of the garden, forced to make a living by the sweat of their brow and the labor of their hands. They and their descendants began offering sacrifices to Him and calling upon Him in prayer.[1] In fact, Genesis 4:26 says it was not until the birth of Adam's grandson Enos that men began *"to call upon the name of the LORD."* The Bible says Adam was one hundred and thirty years old when Seth was born (see Genesis 5:3), and Seth was one hundred and five years old when his son Enos was born (see Genesis 5:6). So for over two hundred years, despite the Fall, men and women did not find it necessary to call on God by name. They were still that aware of His presence.

> For centuries, people did not know the name of God.

I often wish that we could regain that intimate state of communion with the Lord! In my own prayer life, I have felt very near to Him at times—so near that it was not necessary to offer Him any formal prayer. It was enough just to be in His presence. The Bible says, *"Draw nigh to God, and he will draw nigh to you"* (James 4:8), and that's the kind of experience He has given me in prayer. Yet none of us has regained the depth of intimacy with the Lord that would let us worship Him heart-to-heart, as Adam's family did.

Paul knew that one day he would meet God. He affirmed, *"Then shall I know even as also I am known"* (1 Corinthians 13:12). All of us look forward to such a day. But for now we are limited by our human imperfections and the distractions of this carnal world. We must shut the door of our prayer closets and focus our thoughts on God if we are to have any fellowship with Him. The human race has needed to pray this way ever since the days of Enos.

Humankind fell into deep corruption in the centuries that followed Adam. Finally, God had to destroy most of the human race with a worldwide flood, saving only a godly man named Noah and his family in one last effort to salvage humanity. The Bible says that when the flood waters receded and Noah's great wooden ark came to rest on Mount Ararat, he left the ark to build an altar and offer sacrifices to God. (See Genesis 8:18–21.) He wanted to make a fresh beginning for the human race, and he started by worshipping God.

What's in a Name?

Centuries later, God spoke to a godly man named Abram and invited him to leave his native homeland (in what is now Iran) and travel to Canaan. As soon as Abram arrived in that land, he also built an altar and offered sacrifices to God. (See Genesis 12:7.)

Notice how important the worship of God was to these men. Each of them celebrated the landmark event of his life by building an altar, burning a sacrifice on it, and uttering praise to God. Worship was a way of life for them. Yet God had to remind them who He was again and again.

He put a rainbow in the sky to remind Noah that He was a benevolent God and would never again destroy the earth with water. (See Genesis 9:14–17.) When Abram worshipped Him, He said, *"Fear not, Abram: I am thy shield, and thy exceeding great reward"* (Genesis 15:1). He also said, *"I am the LORD that brought thee out of Ur of the Chaldees, to give thee this land to inherit it"* (Genesis 15:7). Finally He said, *"I am the Almighty God; walk before me, and be thou perfect"* (Genesis 17:1). It was as if God had to present His credentials every time He talked with them because they kept forgetting who He was.

"The God My Folks Worshipped"

When Abraham's grandson Jacob dreamed of a ladder reaching to the throne of heaven, God said to him, *"I am the LORD God of Abraham thy father, and the God of Isaac*

[Jacob's immediate father]: *the land whereon thou liest, to thee will I give it, and to thy seed*" (Genesis 28:13).[2] God had already promised the land to Abraham and his descendants; now He would fulfill that promise to Jacob and his immediate family.

But God had to keep reminding Jacob of who He was. When Jacob went to work for his Uncle Laban in the land of Haran, God spoke to him in another dream and said, "*I am the God of Bethel, where thou anointedst the pillar, and where thou vowedst a vow unto me: now arise, get thee out from this land, and return unto the land of thy kindred*" (Genesis 31:13).[3] Yet when Jacob talked about God, notice how he referred to Him: "*the God of my father, the God of Abraham, and the fear of Isaac*" (Genesis 31:42) and "*the God of Abraham, and the God of Nahor, the God of their father*" (Genesis 31:53).

> God had to keep reminding Jacob of who He was.

If Jacob ever knew God's name, he seems to have forgotten it! He referred to Him only as "the God my folks always worshipped."

I'm afraid this is the only way many people identify God today. "Sure, I know God," they say. "My folks have worshipped Him for years. He and I are not personal friends, but He's a good friend of my parents." Yet there is a world of difference between knowing God and knowing *about* God. Someone who knows Him only as "the God my folks worshipped" simply knows *about* Him. We need to become so intimately acquainted with God that we fall on our knees and say with Thomas, *"My Lord and my God"* (John 20:28).

Of course, Jacob may have referred to God as "the God of Abraham and Isaac" as a gesture of respect. He may have been underscoring the fact that God had been faithful to his forefathers and was also faithful to him. Some Bible commentators interpret Jacob's words this way.

But I think Jacob's spiritual "track record" says otherwise. He was a cunning, deceitful man who tricked his older brother out of his birthright and made off with part of his uncle's flocks. Only in times of crisis did Jacob turn to God. Jacob's brother Esau learned he was coming home and went out to meet him. Jacob was desperate. He wailed to the *"God of my father Abraham, and God of my father Isaac, the* LORD *which saidst unto me, Return unto thy country"* (Genesis 32:9). Jacob was still on very formal terms with God, not friendly terms.

Only after Jacob's faith had been <u>tested</u> a great deal more, did God appear to him again and say, *"Thy name shall not be called any more Jacob, but Israel shall be thy name"* (Genesis 35:10). The Hebrew name *Israel* literally means "ruling with God."

And God said unto him, I am God Almighty: be fruitful and multiply; a nation and a company of nations shall be of thee, and kings shall come out of thy loins. (Genesis 35:11)[4]

Not only did God give Jacob a new name, but He revealed more of His own divine nature to him. He revealed that He was all-powerful and able to do anything He promised to do. So His vow to bring *"a nation and a company of nations"* out of this man was no casual promise.

It carried the authority of an omnipotent God, a God whom Jacob had come to trust.

"TELL THEM 'I AM THAT I AM' SENT YOU"

I am giving you a quick review of God's early relationship with humanity so that you can see how individuals tried to perceive God. Sometimes people had a special name for God (as we'll see in the following chapters); sometimes they could only refer to God in terms of something He had done for them. Through it all, humankind was reaching out to God, trying to understand who He was and that He should be worshipped. We see this occurring most vividly about four hundred years after the death of Jacob (or Israel), when God called a man named Moses to lead Jacob's descendants out of Egypt.

Moses himself was an Israelite who fled from Egypt after he murdered a government official. He was tending

14

✗ NO! God was the one reaching to humankind by progressively revealing who He IS the flocks of his father-in-law in the craggy wastelands of the Sinai Peninsula when God appeared to him. To make sure that Moses recognized Him for who He was, God appeared in a bush that burned without being consumed. That sight was bound to attract a shepherd's attention! So Moses said, *"I will now turn aside, and see this great sight, why the bush is not burnt"* (Exodus 3:3). And as he came near to the bush, he heard God in the midst of it, saying, *"Put off thy shoes from off thy feet, for the place whereon thou standest is holy ground"* (Exodus 3:5).

God explained to Moses that He had appeared previously to Abraham, Isaac, and Jacob (verse 6). Then He gave Moses the task of returning to Egypt and confronting the Pharaoh himself to demand the release of the Israelite slaves.

> *Moses wanted to know God's name because the name would tell him something about the very nature of God.*

Moses was scared. He tried to make excuses to God. He said, *"Behold, when I come unto the children of Israel, and shall say unto them, The God of your fathers hath sent me unto you; and they shall say to me, What is his name? what shall I say unto them?"* (verse 13). Here was the supreme test of God's intentions. If God really meant business with Moses, He would reveal His name. Otherwise, Moses

15

would know the relationship with God was only casual. He would only be able to know God "at a distance," and perhaps God would leave him when the going got tough.

But God gave Moses a name for Himself. He said, *"Thus shalt thou say unto the children of Israel, I AM hath sent me unto you"* (Exodus 3:14). The Hebrew word *(yhwh)* that God gave him is a puzzle, even to Bible scholars today. It has no clear-cut, simple translation. The closest it has been translated is "I am who I am." In the next chapter, we'll explore what these words conveyed to the Israelites when Moses carried the message to them. But notice how eager Moses was to identify God. He wanted to know God's name because the name would tell him something about the very nature of God.

A NAME, NOT A "HANDLE"

Several major highways converge in South Bend. We get a large amount of heavy truck traffic through our city, some going right past the Christian Center where I pastor. The truckers have developed their own special jargon for us on the citizens' band radio, and I overhear them using some of that CB lingo at local restaurants.

A very common CB term is "handle." Truckers use that word when they want to get the name another trucker goes by. They say, "What's your handle?"

I suppose they use "handle" because that's what a name does for them; it lets them get hold of someone they know. To use that old cliché, a name lets them "get a han-dle" on their friends.

If you ever visit the Philippines and hear the jungle tribesmen call upon their gods for help, you'll discover that the names of the gods are supposed to have magic power. These people believe that when they invoke the name of a certain god, he must come and do their bid-ding—whether or not he wants to! Like many pagans, they believe a god is a kind of supernatural serving boy who will jump to help them the moment they snap their fingers.

> God is the Ruler of the universe, who expects us to serve Him — not the other way around!!

But the true God is not like that. He is the sovereign Ruler of the universe, who expects us to serve Him—not the other way around! So when we call upon the name of God, we are using a "handle" to bring Him to us. He will help us only if we have followed His commandments; He will put His promises into effect only if we have met the conditions of those promises.

On the Day of Pentecost, Peter said, *"Whosoever shall call on the name of the Lord shall be saved"* (Acts 2:21). Three thousand people did. When the apostles Peter and John met a lame man at the gate of the temple, Peter said,

"In the name of Jesus Christ of Nazareth rise up and walk" (Acts 3:6), and the man did. Peter's testimony was that *"through faith in his name* [Jesus] *hath made this man strong"* (Acts 3:16). Later the apostles asked God *"that signs and wonders may be done by the name of thy holy child Jesus"* (Acts 4:30), and an earthquake shook the place where they were assembled (verse 31).

This was no magic. These men were not ordering God around by using His "handle." Not by any means! They received God's blessing only because they were obedient to God in every way, including the manner in which they prayed. God instructed them to pray in His name; that's what we are expected to do as followers of Jesus Christ. But that in itself would not force God to do something against His will, nor would it force Him to bless someone unworthy of a blessing.

When the Israelites fled to the shore of the Red Sea, Moses commanded them to stand still and called upon the Lord to fight back the pursuing Egyptian army. God did not do what Moses asked, however, because He had a better plan in mind. *"And the LORD said unto Moses, Wherefore criest thou unto me? speak unto the children of Israel, that they go forward"* (Exodus 14:15). So Moses urged his people to run toward the sea itself, and God divided the waters so they could pass through on dry ground.

When the pagan armies of Ai defeated the Israelites, Joshua threw himself on the ground and said,

Alas, O Lord God, wherefore hast thou at all brought this people over Jordan, to deliver us into the hand of the Amorites, to destroy us? would to God we had been content, and dwelt on the other side Jordan! O Lord, what shall I say, when Israel turneth their backs before their enemies! (Joshua 7:7–8)

But God saw the situation differently.

And the LORD said unto Joshua, Get thee up; wherefore liest thou thus upon thy face? Israel hath sinned, and they have also transgressed my covenant which I commanded them: for they have even taken of the accursed thing, and have also stolen, and dissembled also, and they have put it even among their own stuff. Therefore the children of Israel could not stand before their enemies, but turned their backs before their enemies, because they were accursed: neither will I be with you any more, except ye destroy the accursed from among you. (verses 10–12)

God refuses to bless people who are clinging to their sins. As a pastor, I talk with many people who expect God to treat them kindly, even though they often disobey Him. They seem to think that God is a kind of "Daddy Warbucks" who will give them everything they desire, no matter what they do. But they are wrong. God is not a "soft touch." He is not deceived by the glib tongues of people who promise Him the moon but fail to deliver. He is not a foolish God.

He blesses people if they meet His conditions, not just because they call upon Him. As Billy Graham says:

> There is one thing God's love cannot do. It cannot forgive the unrepentant sinner...God will not force Himself on any man against his will. A person can hear a message about the love of God and say, "No, I won't have it," and God will let him go on in his sin to slavery and judgment.[5]

So it is with the prayer of a disobedient person. That person may plead with God and try to claim the promises of God. As long as he or she disobeys God, however, that individual can expect no help, God will not be ordered around by the whims of man. He will not put aside His own will to do our will.

A BLESSING, NOT A CURSE

While some people use God's name in prayer, others use His name in cursing. They seem to think that God's name adds weight to their temper tantrums. It doesn't; in fact, it shows how little they know of God.

If those who curse in God's name really knew Him, they would know that He said, *"Thou shalt not take the name of the LORD thy God in vain; for the LORD will not hold him guiltless that taketh his name in vain"* (Exodus 20:7). This is one of the most commonly violated of the Ten Commandments because people do not know what it means.

The word *vain* normally means "selfish pride" or "conceit." When we say that a person is vain, we mean this person is puffed up with pride. This is an arrogant kind of attitude that says, "I'm better than everyone else."

To "take the Lord's name in vain," means to use His name for your own selfish purposes. Some people swear oaths casually in God's name, as if God lent His authority to their word. They say, "God knows that I've done thus-and-so." What vanity! Others exclaim, "Oh God!" at the slightest provocation, as if they were on chummy terms with Him. What conceit! Still others angrily tell God to damn someone or something that irritates them at the moment, as if God were taking orders from them. What blasphemous pride!

> *This is an arrogant kind of attitude that says, "I'm better than everyone else."*

But there is another, more subtle kind of "taking God's name in vain"—a kind many Christians practice. That is the vain habit of pronouncing God's condemnation against something that God does not condemn. Some Christians—including some preachers—denounce in God's name things they don't happen to like.

For example, I remember a time when many preachers denounced the cutting of a woman's hair; they said it was a worldly, sinful practice. Some preachers harangued their people about the "sin" of drinking coffee or tea. Others railed about women who wore lipstick; they said it was a *"superfluity of naughtiness"* (James 1:21).

Now there's nothing wrong with denouncing sin, as long as God's Word really says it is sin. But when you try to distort God's Word to make *everything that you don't like* a sin, you are using God's name in vain, just as much as the infidel who swears the most vile oaths in God's name. Bible commentator Bo Reicke summed it up well:

> Unhappily the tongue of many pretended Christians (James 3:9–10) has assumed a double function. With the same tongue believers bless God and curse men, who are created in the image of God...In their eagerness to appear as prophets of doom they believe that it is part of the Christian message to pronounce curses upon degraded mankind...There is an absolute difference in kind between the true Christian message and the expression of the poisonous tongue. Bitter dissatisfaction has nothing to do with the gospel, and it is impossible to oscillate between the one and the other.[6]

God's name is a word of blessing not a curse. We should never invoke God's name to accomplish our own selfish ends, even if we can think of some "good" reason to justify it. God's name is holy. It should be spoken reverently. It should be invoked only for the most godly purposes. God's name should not be a part of someone's "gutter talk." It also should not be the high-caliber "shell" that explodes in some preacher's barrage against his personal peeves. God's name is meant to bring hope, healing, and happiness to all people. Let's be sure we use His name to that end.

"TELL ME THAT NAME AGAIN"

This book discusses some of the Hebrew names for God, names used in the Old Testament. But we should also take a brief look at the names of God's Son, Jesus Christ, who is God incarnate, God in the flesh. The names of Jesus tell us a great deal about His character as He ministered on this earth. We can draw a great deal of comfort from meditating upon the names of Jesus because they remind us again of His deep love for us. Bill and Gloria Gaither penned these beautiful lines:

> Jesus, Jesus, Jesus!
> There's just something about that name!
> Master, Savior, Jesus!
> Like the fragrance after the rain.*

And that should be the testimony of every Christian, should it not? There's no earthly name to compare with the name of our precious Jesus, who died to save us from our sins. What then are some of the names that the New Testament uses to refer to Him?

Jesus. The Greek name *Jesus* comes from the Hebrew name *Yeshua,* which means "God the Savior" or "God is salvation." In our English Old Testament, it is the name *Joshua.* This is the name most commonly used in the New Testament to refer to Him. It's the name His mother Mary gave to Him because the angel of God revealed to her that He would *"save his people from their sins"* (Matthew 1:21).

> *Kings and prophets were anointed with holy oil to show that God had chosen them for a special purpose.*

Christ. This Greek name means "the anointed One," and that is also what the Hebrew name *Messiah* means. So when the Bible speaks of "Jesus Christ," it literally means "Jesus the Messiah" or "Our Savior, the Anointed One." In Old Testament times, new kings and prophets were anointed with holy oil to show that God had chosen them for a special purpose. Although Jesus was not (as far as we know) anointed with oil at the beginning of His ministry, He was anointed with God's Holy Spirit. (See Luke 3:21–22.)

Immanuel. In Hebrew, this name means "God (is) with us." The prophet Isaiah announced that the promised Messiah of God would be called by this name (see Isaiah 7:14), indicating that He would be God in the flesh.

Matthew says that Jesus fulfilled this prophecy (see Matthew 1:23), although He was not commonly called by this name. Perhaps this was because the average Jew of Jesus' day was not able to grasp the miracle of the Incarnation.

Master. The New Testament records that Jesus' disciples called Him by several Greek names that the King James Version translates as "Master." The most common of these was *didaskalos,* meaning "Teacher." Another was *kurios*, meaning "lord" or "overseer." The gospel of Matthew tells us that a certain scribe once came to Jesus and said, *"Master [didaskalos], I will follow thee whithersoever thou goest"* (Matthew 8:19). Jesus replied, *"The foxes have holes, and the birds of the air have nests; but the Son of man hath not where to lay his head"* (verse 20). Jesus knew that if this man thought He was merely a great teacher about to form a prestigious corps of Jewish scholars, the man would be greatly disappointed. Jesus and His followers were destined to suffer and even die for the truth He came to proclaim.

Paul, in his letter to the Colossians, said, *"Masters, give unto your servants that which is just and equal; knowing that ye also have a Master [kurios] in heaven"* (Colossians 4:1). He portrayed Jesus as a just and compassionate Master who provides the most basic needs of His servants.

Son of God. When the angel appeared to Mary and predicted Jesus' birth, he said, *"That Holy One who is to be born will be called the Son of God"* (Luke 1:35 NKJV).

Jesus' followers often addressed Him as "the Son of God" (compare Matthew 16:16; John 11:27). So did unbelievers (see Mark 14:61), and even demons. (See Luke 4:41.)

Son of Man. Jesus most often used this name to refer to Himself. He was keenly aware of being both God and man, and perhaps wanted to stress the reality of His incarnation to all who heard Him. Even though He called Himself the "Son of man," Jesus did not hide the fact of His divine nature and power. For example, as Jesus foretold the end times, He said, *"Then shall all the tribes of the earth mourn, and they shall see the Son of man coming in the clouds of heaven with power and great glory"* (Matthew 24:30). Surely He was no ordinary man! He was and is, at once, both God and Man.

> Job looked forward to the day when his Messiah would purchase his soul's release from death.

Redeemer. We often use this name to refer to Jesus, but did you know it is not used in the New Testament? It is only found in the Old. The Hebrew word *gaal* ("redeemer") literally means "one who redeems someone from jail." Job looked forward to the day when his Messiah would purchase his soul's release from death. He said, *"For I know that my redeemer liveth, and that he shall stand at the latter day upon the earth"* (Job 19:25). He was referring, of course, to Jesus Christ.

The Bible has many other names for Jesus, each one revealing a bit more of His unique character and ministry. We don't have space to examine all of them, but I thought you might like this brief background on some of the more familiar names for Jesus. He is, after all, the eternal Son of God in human flesh. So the names of Jesus are names of the Son of God. They tell us something about the One who came to reveal God the Father.

UNLOCKING THE TREASURE

Bible students have long been fascinated by the unique role of names in the Scriptures. Perhaps names have little importance to today's man on the street, but they had great importance to the people living at the time the Bible was written. In the introduction to Robert Young's well-known *Analytical Concordance to the Bible,* we find this interesting comment:

> In Scripture, a name is much more than an identifying tag. It denotes the essence and character of a person or thing. Jesus told His disciples, "And he shall be hated of all men for my Name's sake...." Surely Christians were persecuted for more than the literal name of Jesus. Similarly, the psalmist often refers to those who love "the name of the Lord" (e.g.,

Psalm 5:11), but it would be ridiculous to think that someone could love the name of the Lord without loving the Lord Himself.[7]

In over sixty years of evangelistic work, I have done considerable Bible study. Again and again, I am surprised to find new insights as I examine the names of God. Each name is like a golden key, ready to unlock a treasure of truth to the inquiring mind.

Thus, in the following pages I want to share some of the discoveries I have made in my studies. My goal is not to make you a biblical "egghead," spouting off Hebrew phrases to impress your friends. Vanity is not my purpose, and it should not be yours. But I trust you will draw closer to the Lord Himself as you learn more about Him through this study. And if you have not yet become a newborn child of God through the saving blood of His Son, Jesus Christ, I pray this volume will inspire you to take that step.

NOTES

1. The Bible does not specifically say that Adam and Eve offered sacrifices to God. The Bible first records sacrifices made by their sons, Cain and Abel. (See Genesis 4.) But we must assume that the parents taught their sons about God and showed them how to worship Him.

2. God gave Abram a new name, Abraham, literally meaning "father of a multitude" (Genesis 17:5). Obviously, God saw great significance in a name!

3. When Jacob woke up from his dream of the ladder, he set up a stone pillar and worshipped the Lord there, calling it *Beth-el* (literally, "house of God").

4. In chapter 5, we will see that this phrase "God Almighty" actually became a Hebrew name for God.

5. Billy Graham, *Till Armageddon: A Perspective on Suffering* (Waco, Tex.: Word Books, 1981), pp. 46–47.

6. Bo Reicke, "The Epistles of James, Peter, and Jude," *The Anchor Bible*, Vol. 37 (Garden City, N.Y.: Doubleday and Company, 1964), pp. 39–40.

7. Robert Young, *Young's Analytical Concordance to the Bible*, Revelation by William B. Stevenson and David Wimbish (Nashville: Thomas Nelson Publishers, 1980), p. vii.

CHAPTER 2

THE LORD
(YAHWEH/JEHOVAH)

I AM

I n the first chapter, we saw that God told Moses, *"Thus shalt thou say unto the children of Israel, I AM hath sent me unto you"* (Exodus 3:14). The Hebrew name that God used to identify Himself here, as we have mentioned, is a puzzle and a mystery to Bible scholars even today. There is no other name like it in all of the ancient Hebrew literature. And the Jewish scribes who copied the manuscripts of the Bible felt the name was so holy that they did not even pronounce it. They wrote it without the vowels, because it was never to be spoken aloud.

Whenever you find the name *LORD* written in small capitals like this in the King James Version of the Bible, it represents this name that God revealed to Moses. The Bible first records this name in Genesis 2:4. Moses wrote the first five books of the Bible (sometimes called the Pentateuch), probably during the forty years that the Israelites wandered in the wilderness. By that time, he knew this intriguing name of God, so Moses used it to record the very earliest history of the human race in Genesis.

What clues do we have to the meaning of this mysterious name? First, the Hebrew manuscripts tell us that the consonants of the name were YHWH. That's all. We don't know for sure what vowels were supposed to be inserted in that word; it could have been pronounced "Yowoh" or "Yehwah" or several other ways. Bishop Clement of Alexandria, writing in the third century A.D., noted that the name was pronounced "Yaoweh." Theodoret of Cyprus, a century later, said that the Samaritans pronounced it "Yabeh." Third-century manuscripts found in Egypt confirm this latter pronunciation.[1] Based on such information, scholars have come to assume that the name of God was pronounced "Yahweh."

> The Hebrew name God used to identify Himself is a puzzle and a mystery to scholars.

But if the Jews thought this name was too holy to pronounce, what did they do when they read the Scriptures aloud? Did they just skip the name of God?

No, they took the vowels from the Hebrew name Adonai ("Lord") and inserted them in the name YHWH to make *YaHoWaH*. (This is pronounced as "Jehovah.") Since this word is really a combination of the Hebrew names for "God" and "Lord," we can safely say that it means "Lord God."

So much for this little excursion into the mechanics of Hebrew. We still have a tough question to answer: What does the name mean?

The word Yahweh came from a Hebrew verb that means "to be." The name appears to have meant "I AM." That seems very simple. But think about the deep implications of that simple name.

THE GOD WHO ALWAYS IS

The Bible tells how Abraham made a covenant with Abimelech, a ruler of the Canaanites, because Abimelech saw that God blessed everything Abraham did. (See Genesis 21:22.) As a part of their treaty, Abimelech agreed to return to Abraham what he had stolen from him. So they called the place *Beersheba*, meaning "well of the oath." The Bible says that Abraham planted a grove of trees at that place as a memorial to their treaty, *"and called there on the name of the LORD, the everlasting God"* (Genesis 21:33).

God told Moses that He was the God who always had been, and who always would be. He was the eternal God. No matter what might happen in the world, and even in the entire universe, God would continue to live and reign as God. In his notes to *The Criswell Study Bible,* Dr. W. A. Criswell comments:

> God exists in a way that no one or anything else does. His [supreme] nature is implied by His ever-present existence without beginning or ending. He is the only God who exists, and all other existence is dependent upon His uncaused existence.[2]

✓ The other nations of Moses' day worshipped perishable gods. Egypt, the most powerful nation in that part of the world, worshipped animals such as monkeys, alligators, cats—even beetles! The Egyptians thought these animals and insects represented the gods of the universe. For instance, the falcon represented Re, the sun god. When one of these animals died, it was given a very stately burial. Archaeologists have found thousands of cat mummies, bird mummies, and mummies of other animals considered sacred. The Egyptians *worshipped* these things. Yet their gods perished, as did they, or as they also perished.

Imagine how radical Moses' message to his people must have been! He returned to Egypt from the sun-parched wilderness of the Sinai to tell the Israelites, "I AM has sent me." The God who had always lived and always would live—who had always been God and always would be God—had sent Moses.

The message was startling then, and it's just as startling today.

America worships the present day. Television commercials try to convince us that any new product must be better than all of the competition. Political leaders scour the country for new faces every election year, hoping to attract voters with their "new-and-improved" candidates. Families plan their budgets one week at a time (if they plan at all), because they think the present is all that matters. That's the mind-set of modern America: Live today to the fullest, for there may be no tomorrow.

> *That's the mind-set of modern America: Live today to the fullest, for there may be no tomorrow.*

Therefore, present-day Americans are reluctant to follow an eternal God. They feel uncomfortable with the idea that God stakes His claim on all of our future plans, as well as today's. They don't like a long-term commitment to anyone; they certainly don't want to worship anyone. These people want a disposable way of life, one they can rearrange or discard at their slightest whim. So they sneer at the Bible-preaching ministers of *Yahweh,* just as the Israelite slaves must have sneered at Moses when he came to promise their deliverance. An unchanging God? An everlasting covenant with

35

*** no, don't want to submitt

* I don't think that.

** not that they dislike, but are afraid

God? A lifelong commitment to God? Why, that sounds like a foreign language! Yet that is the claim placed upon our lives by the great "I AM." And He has a right!

The Self-Sufficient God

God was never created by some greater power. He was never conjured up by some human mind. He depends upon no one and nothing to continue living; He will live forever. One Bible commentator explains it this way:

> *"I AM THAT I AM"* signifies that He is self-existent, the only real being and the source of all reality; that He is self- sufficient.[3]

We human beings may talk of being self-sufficient, but we don't know what that really means. During the early years of this nation, settlers pushed into the forests of Appalachia to build crude log cabins and to carve little farms out of the wilderness. They felt self-sufficient. But the family members still depended on one another to make clothes, cut firewood, draw water, harvest crops, and do all the things necessary to sustain life. The pioneers were not really self-sufficient.

Today we read of young families who have abandoned urban life to go "back to nature." They have bought little tracts of land in the forest, just as their ancestors did. Now they are building solar-heated log cabins and they are raising hybrid vegetables. But still they are not self-sufficient.

They depend on one another—and on those of us who have remained in the cities—to provide these supplies they need to build their homes.

Individuals depend upon other individuals, families upon other families, and nations upon other nations. But God depends upon no one. He never gets hungry or shivers in the cold. He will never die of old age or suffer for lack of medical help. He is God! *Hallelujah* !

The Real God

Religious hucksters have invaded human society. Fakes, quacks, and charlatans set up false gods, or make false claims about the true God, to make a reputation for themselves and reap a handsome profit. Self-professed healers often demand that people pay them large sums of money before they pray for their victims' healing. Money-grabbing "gurus" use every sort of gimmick imaginable to reap profits from their ministry. They succeed because man is so desperate to find the one true God, and to follow Him.

The God who spoke to Moses out of the burning bush was real. He said His name is "I AM," not "I am supposed to be" or "Some people think I am." God needs no one to make extravagant claims for Him. He doesn't need to be sold, glamorized, or promoted by anyone. He will be worshipped for what He is, not for the image that someone may fabricate of Him.

When the Russian cosmonaut Yuri Gagarin peered out through the window of his space capsule into the depths of space, he said he did not see God. He felt his failure to see God was a vindication of his atheistic belief that God is a figment of the capitalist imagination, a fable used to pacify the working class. The communist leaders of Russia ridiculed our faith because they thought it was just make-believe. They said, "If there really were a God, we could see and touch Him. But we can't. So He must not be real."

> People's minds are clouded by unbelief that they can't search for God with any objectivity.

The minds of such people are so clouded by unbelief that they cannot search for God with any objectivity. But if they could put aside their prejudices, they would notice that many things in our world cannot be seen, touched, or measured with instruments. Yet we know these things exist.

Take the force of gravity, for instance. No one would say that gravity is just a fairy tale, but who can *see* gravity? Sure, we see the *effects* of gravity every day. If you trip over a rock, you fall on your face. If you let go of a bag of groceries, it falls to the ground. If you nudge your telephone off the edge of your desk, it falls. In space travel, the effect of gravity—acceleration—is measured in "g's." When we see these things, we know that the force of gravity is at work. But we cannot see gravity itself. We can't touch it. We can't detect it even on the most sophisticated sensing devices. We can only watch its effects.

Likewise, we cannot see, touch, or measure God—but we can see the effects of His activity in our world. We can see people's lives transformed when they surrender themselves to Him. We can see miracles of healing. We can watch the marvelous cycles of the natural world, which keeps renewing itself and preserving itself year after year as if guided by some unseen Person. Yes, we see the effects of God's actions. We know by His revealed Word that they are the results of His activity. So we know that He is real.

Moses had no doubt about that. Moses had never read one word of Holy Scripture (because none had yet been written), but he could see the flames engulfing that bush. He had never heard a sermon, yet he could hear the voice of God. He could hardly remember the testimony of his ancestors who had seen God at work, yet he saw God perform mighty miracles before his own eyes. This was enough to convince Moses that God was no figment of his imagination. As God said, "I AM."

THE UNCHANGEABLE GOD

In my boyhood home of Louisiana, we referred to a very old person by saying, "He's as old as the hills." That was just a figure of speech, of course; no human being is as old as the mountains.

But God is. In fact, He is much older than the mountains because He "Is" from everlasting to everlasting. He made the hills!

People change with age. Their hair turns gray and falls out; their skin wrinkles and toughens; their bones become brittle. And every person will eventually die.

> There was never a time when God the Father, Son, and Holy Spirit was not.

We may not realize it, but the "hills" are always changing, too. Geologists say that the mountains are shifting and buckling under the pressure of great forces within the earth. Wind, rain, and ice wear the mountains away. Man's earthmoving machines whittle away the mountain's profile to make a highway or a shopping center. Every hill changes with age.

But God is older than any human being. He is older than any of the hills. In fact, God is *from everlasting to everlasting* (Psalm 90:2). There was never a time when God the Father, Son, and Holy Spirit was not. And God never changes. He just "IS."

This is hard enough to comprehend concerning the Father. But consider for a moment how this applies to Jesus, and the truth of God's name *Yahweh* becomes even more awesome. Jesus is the second person of the triune, or threefold, God. So when the Bible says God is *"from everlasting to everlasting,"* it also means that Jesus Christ exists *"from everlasting to everlasting."* The eternal Son of the Father has lived since the very beginning and will live forever. The Bible says of Him:

> *In the beginning was the Word, and the Word was with God, and the Word was God. The same was in the beginning with God...He was in the world, and the world was made by him, and the world knew him not. He came unto his own, and his own received him not.* (John 1:1–2, 10–11)

We can hardly imagine how anyone could reject God in human flesh. Jesus was a common man, a neighbor; but He was also the everlasting God. Yet many of Jesus' kinsmen did exactly that. They rejected Him. They spat upon Him. They demanded that He be crucified.

> *But as many as received him, to them gave he power to become the sons of God, even to them that believe on his name: which were born, not of blood, nor of the will of the flesh, nor of the will of man, but of God. And the Word was made flesh, and dwelt among us, (and we beheld his glory).* (John 1:12–14)

Jesus Christ is *Yahweh,* the God who "IS" from endless time before and beyond all time to come. He is our Master and Savior forever.

And the Holy Spirit exists from eternity to eternity. There never was and there never will be a time when He does not proceed eternally from the Father. In fact, Jesus offers Himself to the Father through the "eternal Spirit":

> *How much more shall the blood of Christ, who through the eternal Spirit offered himself without spot to God, purge your conscience from dead works to serve the living God?* (Hebrews 9:14)

THE SELF-FULFILLED GOD

Talk with a college student about career plans, and you'll get some interesting answers. "I'm going to be a physician," says one; "I'm going to be a civil engineer," says another; "I'm going to sell widgets," says a third, and so on. But come back to those same people ten years after they graduate from school, and ask what they have become. The answers will probably be quite different. The "physician" may have become a veterinarian; the "civil engineer" may have become a politician; the "widget salesman" may have become an advertising executive. None of us knows what the future holds for us; that's one of the most exciting and exasperating things about being human.

But there has never been any question about what God the Father, Son, and Holy Spirit would be. God is only what He wills to be—God!

God wills to be righteous, and He is. He wills to be merciful, and He is. He wills to be all-powerful, and He is. Nothing can hinder God from becoming what He wills. He "IS" God, the perfect fulfillment of all that He wills to be.

In the late 1960s and early 1970s, some prominent theologians advocated a new teaching that they called "process theology." The leading thinker of this new movement was the philosopher Alfred North Whitehead. One review of Whitehead's work said:

> His God is not like the God of traditional [Christian belief], a static or perfect Being, but is process. He is becoming so that he has something in common with the living God of biblical faith. But critics...doubt that Whitehead's God can be identified with the God of Christian faith.[4]

I myself certainly doubt Whitehead's ideas. If God were always changing, evolving into some better sort of God, how could we be sure of our relationship with Him? We would live in a nightmare world where we could not trust any of His natural laws. If God intended such anarchy, however, we must discard the Holy Bible. God's Word says concerning the Son that He is *the same yesterday, and to day, and for ever"* (Hebrew 13:8). God's Word is sure. The testimony of God's very name reminds us that He "IS" all that we could ever hope He would be, and all He might ever will to be. He "IS" the fulfillment of His own perfect will. He is not a God "in process," but a perfect, unchanging God. *Amen!*

MUCH REVEALED—MUCH HIDDEN

Despite all of the insights that we can discern through examining God's name *Yahweh,* we must admit that we still do not understand everything about God's character. God's nature is far more mysterious than our minds can completely comprehend. Referring to the title *Yahweh,* one commentator says:

> The name preserves much of His nature hidden from curious and presumptuous enquiry. We cannot by searching find Him out (cf. Proverbs 30:4).[5]

And so it must always be with God. The more of Himself that He reveals to us, the more remains hidden from our view. I'm sure that when Moses withdrew from that burning bush, slipped back into his sandals, and returned to Jethro's flocks, he still had many unanswered questions about God. God promised to go with Moses and his brother, who would act as his translator, when they went back to Egypt. However, there was very little more Moses knew about this One who spoke amidst the flame. But Moses acted on what he did know and obeyed God.

God may be trying to change something in your life. He may be telling you to leave your present job and undertake a new venture that would glorify Him. He may want you to heal a broken relationship in your family. He may call you to surrender an incurable illness to Him so that He can heal you. Whatever He is saying, you may hesitate to obey Him because you want to know more. But you shouldn't hesitate. If God expected us to wait until we understood *everything* about Him, no one would ever serve Him! The human mind has never fully understood God, and never will

> God may be trying to change something in your life.

The apostle Paul said, *"And without controversy great is the mystery of godliness"* (1 Timothy 3:16). Even when he tried to explain the *"deep things of God"* (1 Corinthians 2:10 NKJV), he confessed, *"No one knows the things of God except the Spirit of God"* (verse 11 NKJV). At the end of the familiar "Love Chapter," Paul stated, *"For now we see* [God] *in a mirror, dimly, but then face to face. Now I know in part, but then I shall know just as I also am known"* (1 Corinthians 13:12 NKJV). Yet Paul's lack of complete understanding did not prevent him from doing great things for God. He was ready to obey the heavenly Father despite his incomplete knowledge of Him.

When I give an altar call at the end of a worship service at the Christian Center, people may walk down the aisles to commit their lives to Jesus Christ. Yet if I asked those people to explain the Trinity, the Incarnation, or some other deep truth of God, they probably couldn't do so! That's all right. The church has always called these things "mysteries." Thank God. *"By grace you have been saved through faith"* (Ephesians 2:8), and not through knowledge or understanding.

The name *Yahweh* tells us much about God. It leaves much more shrouded in mystery. But like Moses, we don't need to let the mystery keep us from serving God as we ought.

Notes

1. B. W Anderson, "God, Names of," *The Interpreter's Dictionary of the Bible,* Vol. 2 (Nashville: Abingdon Press, 1962), p. 409.

2. W. A. Criswell, ed., *The Criswell Study Bible* (Nashville: Thomas Nelson Publishers, 1979), p. 75.

3. Francis Davidson, ed., *The New Bible Commentary* (Grand Rapids, Mich.: William B. Eerdmans Publishing Company, 1954), p. 109.

4. William E. Hordern, *A Layman's Guide to Protestant Theology* (New York: The Macmillan Company, 1968), p. 248.

5. Davidson, p. 15.

CHAPTER 3

THE LORD IS GOD
(JEHOVAH-ELOHIM)

The Plural of majesty

One verse of the Creation account has puzzled and intrigued many Bible readers, because it shows that God is more than one person. That verse is Genesis 1:26:

> *And God said, Let **us** make man in **our** image, after **our** likeness: and let them have dominion over the fish of the sea, and over the fowl of the air.*
>
> (emphasis added)

We Christians understand that "us" and "our" refer to the Trinity. The verse reveals that God is three persons in one nature—Father, Son, and Holy Spirit. In Old Testament times, before the birth of Jesus Christ, people did not understand in the way we do today that God is one nature in three persons. But they did know that God was more than one person.

The name He used to identify Himself was *Elohim* (pronounced "el-o-HEEM"). This is a name "reflecting divine majesty and power."[1] In fact, Bible scholars often call it the "plural of majesty."[2] The Bible sometimes uses the word *elohim* to refer to any number of "gods," such as the pagan gods of the Canaanites. (See Exodus 20:3.) But most often *Elohim* is a proper name for the one true God, suggesting His unique nature as the three-in-one God. Yet the name means more than this.

MERCY VERSUS JUSTICE!

The Jewish scholar Samuel Sandmel says, "The ancient rabbis...had asserted that Elohim emphasized God's mercy, while Yahve [*Yahweh*] emphasized His strict justice."[3] The ancient rabbis came to this conclusion after comparing passages in the Bible that use the name *Yahweh* with other passages that use the name *Elohim*. Here are some comparisons:

Yahweh

And the LORD [Yahweh] said, My spirit shall not always strive with man, for that he also is flesh: yet his days shall be an hundred and twenty years.
(Genesis 6:3)

And, behold, the word of the LORD [Yahweh] came unto him, saying, This [Ishmael] shall not be thine heir; but he that shall come forth out of thine own bowels shall be thine heir.   (Genesis 15:4)

And Laban said unto him, I pray thee, if I have found favour in thine eyes, tarry: for I have learned by experience that the Lord [Yahweh] hath blessed me for thy sake.   (Genesis 30:27)

Elohim

And God [Elohim] blessed them, and God said unto them, Be fruitful, and multiply, and replenish the earth, and subdue it.   (Genesis 1:28)

And Abram fell on his face: and God [Elohim] talked with him, saying...And I will make thee exceeding fruitful, and I will make nations of thee, and kings shall come out of thee.   (Genesis 17:3, 6)

And God hearkened unto Leah, and she conceived.   (Genesis 30:17)

There does seem to be a contrast between those passages that use *Yahweh* and those that use *Elohim*. But we could quote many other verses that stress God's mercy and call Him *Yahweh*, alongside with other verses that stress His justice and call Him *Elohim*. So the rabbis' theory about these names, although there is some truth to it, does not seem completely accurate.

Then what does the name *Elohim* mean, as far as God is concerned? Why call Him *Elohim* when so many other names might be used?

A GOD WORTHY OF WORSHIP

I gave you a clue to the answer at the very beginning of this chapter when I mentioned that the name *elohim* referred to the pagan gods of Old Testament times. *Elohim* basically means "something (or someone) that is worshipped." The *elohim* were the things most revered and honored by ancient man.

> *The elohim were the things most revered and honored by ancient man.*

Most ancient peoples worshipped false gods. For example, the Canaanites worshipped bulls and lambs because they thought these animals were fertility gods. The Canaanites wanted plentiful crops and they hoped to bear many children. So they bowed down before symbols of fertility in hopes of becoming fertile. The bulls and lambs they worshipped were their *elohim*.

In a previous chapter, I mentioned how the Egyptians worshipped all sorts of animals and insects. These things were far inferior to God, but they served as the Egyptians' false gods. They were the Egyptians' objects of worship, their *elohim*. When Moses' father-in-law, Jethro, saw God deliver the Israelites from Egypt, he confessed, *"Now I know that the LORD [Yahweh] is greater than all gods [elohim]: for in the thing wherein they dealt proudly he was above them"* (Exodus 18:11). King David said to God, *"And what one nation in the earth is like thy people...which thou redeemedst to thee from Egypt, from the nations and their gods [elohim]?"* (2 Samuel 7:23).

God proved that these pagan idols were false by showing His people that He alone had power. Yet pagan people continued to serve their *elohim:* They continued to worship God's creatures in place of the Creator Himself. And God punished them for their idolatry.

> *For since the creation of the world His invisible attributes are clearly seen, being understood by the things that are made...so that they are without excuse, because, although they knew God, they did not glorify Him as God, nor were thankful, but became futile in their thoughts, and their foolish hearts were darkened. Professing to be wise, they became fools, and changed the glory of the incorruptible God into an image made like corruptible man; and birds and four-footed animals and creeping things. Therefore God also gave them up to uncleanness,...who exchanged the truth of God for the lie, and worshiped and served the creature rather than the Creator, who is blessed forever. Amen.* (Romans 1:20–25 NKJV)[4]

Our modern word *worship* comes from the Old English word, *weorthscipe,* meaning "to attribute worth" to something. That's what the pagan people did to their *elohim;* they believed idols had great power to influence their everyday lives. They boasted about what their idols did for them. They believed their idols could cure diseases, provide food, deliver them from military foes, and do any number of other things. So they bowed the knee to their *elohim,* their "worthy things," and praised all that these idols were supposed to do.

But the Israelites knew that only *Yahweh* is worthy of praise. Only the one true God could do the things these pagans claimed their idols would do. God told the Israelites that He was the true *Elohim,* the only One to be worshipped. In fact, He often referred to Himself as *Jehovah-Elohim,* a name that literally meant "the LORD IS God." Our Bible translators usually render it as simply, "the LORD God." Here are some examples from the Old Testament:

This is the account of the heavens and the earth when they were created, in the day that the LORD God [Jehovah-Elohim] made earth and heaven
(Genesis 2:4 NASB)

The LORD God [Jehovah-Elohim] made tunics of skins for Adam and his wife and clothed them.
(Genesis 3:21 NEB)

[Moses said,] *But as for you and your servants, I know that you do not yet fear the LORD God [Jehovah-Elohim].* (Exodus 9:30 RSV)

Notice that the title *Elohim* ("God," or "One to Be Worshipped") is attached to God's proper name *Jehovah* as if it were a surname. In the English language, many surnames like "Smith," "Cooper," or "Taylor" originated this way. If a man was a blacksmith, his customers began calling him "John the Smith" or "John Smith." If a woman was a barrel-maker (or cooper), they might call her "Jane the Cooper" or "Jane Cooper." So the people of Israel began calling *Yahweh* "LORD the God," or simply "LORD God." The meaning of that name became crystal-clear on Mount Sinai when God gave Moses the first of the Ten Commandments:

> The people of Israel began calling Yahweh "Lord the God," or simply "Lord God."

*Thou shalt not make unto thee any graven image, or any likeness of any thing that is in heaven above, or that is in the earth beneath, or that is in the water under the earth: Thou shalt not bow down thyself to them, nor serve them: for I **the LORD thy God** am a jealous God, visiting the iniquity of the fathers upon the children...and showing mercy unto thousands of them that love me, and keep my commandments.*

(Exodus 20:4–6, emphasis added)

God expects to be worshipped. He is pleased when we worship Him as He ought to be worshipped. But He grows angry with anyone who neglects worshipping Him properly.

A Lost Discipline

We modern Americans have sadly neglected the worship of God. I think it is time for us to confess that worship is a lost discipline here.

The public's casual attitude toward church attendance indicates this neglect. On a typical Sunday morning, you can drive through a suburban community and see most homeowners mowing the lawn, washing the car, playing touch football—doing all sorts of things *except* going to church! Yet if you took the time to question those same people about their spiritual lives, many of them would say they are "church members." Some would even say they are Christians. Yet their Sunday activities prove that they worship other things besides the one true God they profess to worship. They worship the gods of personal pleasure, recreation, and money.

Another indicator of the sad state of our worship habits is the attitudes of people who *do* attend church. Most churchgoers love to hear a professional musician or a well-known author give a testimony. When the sermon begins, however, they lounge back in their seats and doze off to sleep. These desultory church folk like sanctuary "entertainment," but they don't care to have their souls fed.

One reason for this is the sad state of preaching in America. Most pastors are not really proclaiming the Word; they're dishing up predigested pabulum from current devotional magazines, or they are expounding their favorite psychological theories. But *the word of God is quick, and powerful, and sharper than any twoedged sword, piercing even to the dividing asunder of soul and spirit,...and is a discerner of the thoughts and intents of the heart"* (Hebrews 4:12). When Jesus Christ is preached with the power of the Holy Spirit, people can't help but stay awake! They become aware of what the Bible has to say to them. Why, they might even have to leave the room because they can't stand the conviction they feel! The fact that this seldom happens in our churches is a bitter commentary on the shoddiness of American preaching as well as on the indifference of the American churchgoer.

> When Jesus Christ is preached with the power of the Holy Spirit, people can't help but stay awake!

Once, a shipbuilder attended a preaching service of that fiery eighteenth-century evangelist George Whitefield. "I can usually construct a whole ship during a sermon," he said, "but with Whitefield I couldn't even lay the keel." May God give us more preachers who will preach the Word with such force and fervor that they hold the attention of their congregations like that!

Another indicator of the sad state of American worship is the ineffectuality of most prayers. Why aren't more prayers answered? Has God stopped working in the lives of His people? Aren't Christians praying steadfastly enough? Aren't they praying aright? I suspect the problem isn't with God, but with us.

So little time is given to focused, fervent prayer in the typical American worship service! At best, you might hear a five-minute litany of prayer by the pastor, as he runs down the list of sick and needy people in the church. They become no more than "shopping list" prayers. The Bible says that after Jesus ascended into heaven, His disciples returned to Jerusalem and *"continued with one accord in prayer and supplication"* until the Day of Pentecost (Acts 1:14). They prayed constantly until they got what they were waiting for—the power of the Holy Spirit. Their entire worship service was devoted to prayer. Every aspect of their life for those ten days involved prayer. And God answered their prayer.

I believe that revival will come to churches in America only if Christians devote themselves to prayer. Flashy visitation programs won't bring revival, and neither will slick Madison Avenue advertising gimmicks. The only thing that will open the church to a fresh infilling of the Holy Spirit's power is constant, faithful prayer. Yet such prayer is conspicuously absent from most of our worship services.

Dick Eastman of the World Literature Crusade used to hold seminars on prayer. He called prayer time "The Hour That Changes the World." Matthew 26:40 speaks of Jesus' return from His prayer vigil in Gethsemane. When He found Peter sleeping, Jesus said, *"What, could ye not watch with me one hour?"* After Dick read this verse, he wondered what would happen if he dedicated one hour each day to prayer—nothing but prayer. He tried it and began to see remarkable things happen in his ministry. He recommended such prayer to his friends and colleagues, and they too were blessed. Now he travels about the country, holding seminars on prayer. His program is based on the idea that Christ deserves at least one undisturbed hour of our day in prayer.

Think what might happen if Christians spent even half an hour in prayer together on Sundays!

Think what might happen if Christians spent even half an hour in prayer every Sunday when they came together for worship. Why, we might witness another Day of Pentecost—another mighty outpouring of God's Spirit!

I said earlier that I believed worship is a lost discipline for most American Christians. Worship is a discipline, you know. It does not come naturally for carnal human beings. In most church services we are much too concerned about comfortable seating, or the golf game we want to play, or the pot roast that's in the oven to truly focus our thoughts on God. But *worship must be concentrated*. It must be focused. If we intend to "attribute worth" to God, we must put everything else out of our minds and hearts. Archbishop Fenelon, writing in the seventeenth century, grasped this idea when he wrote,

> The love of God...desires that self should be forgotten, that it should be counted as nothing, that God might be all in all. God knows that it is best for us when self is trampled underfoot and broken as an idol, in order that He might live within us, and make us after His will...So let that vain, complaining babbler—self-love—be silenced, that in the stillness of the soul we may listen to God.[5]

HOW TO WORSHIP AS WE OUGHT

If we truly believe that God is *Jehovah-Elohim,* we should start worshipping Him *"in spirit and in truth"* (John 4:23). We should worship Him wholeheartedly. Let me suggest some ways that you can improve your worship to God.

1. *Study the Word of God.* Notice I said, "study," not just "read" the Bible. There's a world of difference between the two. A Bible student comes to the Word of God with a real hunger to learn more of God's will for his life. He reads the Bible prayerfully, thoughtfully, and meditatively. He takes time to absorb what Scripture says and to apply the Word to current problems in his life. Job said, *"I have esteemed the words of his mouth more than my necessary food"* (Job 23:12). The apostle Peter said, *"As newborn babes, desire the sincere milk of the word, that ye may grow thereby"* (1 Peter 2:2). And the Bible gives ample proof that God can use His written Word to bring revival among His people if they will only study it.

> *A Bible student comes to the Word of God with a real hunger to learn more of God's will for his life.*

2. *Obey what you read in the Word of God.* This seems so simple that it almost goes without saying. But the great majority of Christians ignore this simple rule. They read the Bible, then slap the Book closed and walk away.

But be ye doers of the word, and not hearers only, deceiving your own selves. For if any be a hearer of the word, and not a doer, he is like unto a man beholding his natural face in a glass: for he beholdeth himself,

*and goeth his way, and straightway forgetteth what
manner of man he was.*　　　　　　　(James 1:22–24)

If your spiritual life is weak, it may be because you've
disregarded what God's Word admonishes you to do. Begin
obeying Scripture, and you'll be able to worship more free-
ly. You'll be better able to enjoy His presence.

3. *Confess that He is God and you are His servant.*
Again, this seems so simple, but many Christians keep
trying to make themselves God, and to make God their
servant. A. W. Tozer touched on this problem when he
wrote:

> Before the Spirit of God can work creatively in our
> hearts, He must condemn and slay the "flesh" within
> us; that is, He must have our full consent to displace
> our natural self with the Person of Christ...Nothing
> that comes from God will minister to my pride of
> self-congratulation. If I am tempted to be complacent
> and to feel superior because I have had a remarkable
> vision or an advanced spiritual experience, I should
> go at once to my knees and repent of the whole thing.
> I have fallen a victim to the enemy.[6]

When self keeps God off the throne of your life, you are
bound to have a discouraging worship experience because
you are really worshipping yourself instead of God. You
must be able to say with Paul, *"I die daily"* (1 Corinthians

15:31), and *"I am crucified with Christ: nevertheless I live; yet not I, but Christ liveth in me: and the life which I now live in the flesh I live by the faith of the Son of God, who loved me, and gave himself for me"* (Galatians 2:20). We must truly let Christ, not ourselves, reign in our hearts if we want to have a meaningful life of worship.

4. *Make peace with any Christian who is at odds with you.* Jesus said, *"Therefore if thou bring thy gift to the altar, and there rememberest that thy brother hath ought against thee; leave there thy gift before the altar, and go thy way; first be reconciled to thy brother, and then come and offer thy gift"* (Matthew 5:23–24). Did you ever feel that your prayers were getting no higher than the ceiling? Maybe that was because you had a conflict with some other Christian. Jesus said you need to settle your problems with other Christians before you pray at the altar of God—even if you're not the one who's upset. Notice that he said, *"If thy brother hath aught against thee."*

> Make peace with any Christian who is at odds with you.

I wonder what would happen in our Sunday morning worship services if pastors began the prayer time by saying, "We're going to pause for a minute to let you iron out any problems you have with your brothers and sisters here. Then we'll pray." In the worship services of the early church, the kiss of peace always preceded Communion, to give the people the opportunity to make certain they were reconciled to one another. I think we would be pleasantly surprised at what God could do were His people to establish such peace with each other.

5. *Begin your prayer with praise.* So many Christians give the Lord a perfunctory "thank You" at the start of prayer, just as a prelude to the "real" business of *asking* God for things. They remind me of someone who curtly doffs his hat to a stranger and then asks for a handout. God doesn't appreciate that sort of "courtesy"!

Make sure you start your prayer with genuine praise of God. Praise Him for being who He is. Praise Him for what He has done in your life. Praise Him for what He has promised to do in the future. Put your petitions out of your mind for the time being; just focus your thoughts on God and let your praises flow. The psalmist said, *"Enter into his gates with thanksgiving, and into his courts with praise: be thankful unto him, and bless his name"* (Psalm 100:4). That's still good advice.

6. *Make specific prayer requests.* There is a proper time in each prayer for bringing your requests to God—after you have truly praised Him and meditated on who He is. When the time for petitions comes, make sure you are specific. Don't say, "Lord, bless my children." Let Him know *in what way* you believe they need to be blessed. Tell Him

if they need to be saved, healed, aided with their finances, or anything else. Don't say, "Lord, work out this problem that I have." Let Him know *in what way* you need His help in resolving it. Indicate that you've wrestled with this problem and tried to discern His will in the matter before you approached Him with your requests. The Bible says, *"The effectual fervent prayer of a righteous man availeth much"* (James 5:16). That word *effectual* means that you should pray for specific "effects," specific results that you feel are in keeping with the will of God.

> *A vague prayer indicates that you're really not concerned about the outcome of the request.*

A vague, general prayer probably indicates that you're really not too concerned about the outcome of your request.

7. *Make "quiet space" for God.* Modern lifestyles leave little room for quiet meditation, and most of us have forgotten what an hour of silence feels like. A friend of mine once spent a day at a Catholic retreat center to meditate and pray. The first few hours were very uncomfortable, he said. Know why? Because he could hear no radio, television, or telephone! It was called a discipline of silence. "I felt like I was on another planet," he remembered.

The saints of past centuries knew the value of having quiet times with the Lord. They retired to their prayer closets or to a secluded hillside every day just to talk with Him. God told the people of Israel, *"In returning and rest shall ye be saved; in quietness and in confidence shall be your strength: and ye would not"* (Isaiah 30:15). If you will take time to make some "quiet spaces" for meditating, praying, and worshipping God, you will find far more strength in your spirit than you have now.

CALL OTHERS TO WORSHIP

Followers of the ancient Persian cult of Ahura-Mazda believed they should keep their pagan "truth" to themselves, so they did not invite outsiders to their worship services. The same was true of those infamous heretics of the early church, the Gnostics. Other offbeat groups throughout the intervening centuries have tried to keep mystic secrets of their religion to themselves.

But the followers of *Jehovah-Elohim* do just the opposite. They invite their unbelieving friends to join them in worshipping God. In fact, they believe that evangelism— calling others to God—is a key part of their own worship. If He is truly *Elohim,* the One worthy of worship, then all people ought to worship Him.

Thus saith God the LORD, he that created the heavens, and stretched them out; he that spread forth the earth, and that which cometh out of it; he that giveth breath unto the people upon it, and spirit to them that walk therein: I the LORD have called thee in righteousness, and

will hold thine hand, and will keep thee, and give thee
for a covenant of the people, for a light of the Gentiles;
to open the blind eyes, to bring out the prisoners from
the prison....I am the LORD: that is my name: and my
glory will I not give to another, neither my praise to
graven images.   (Isaiah 42:5–8)

We modern-day Christians are tempted to think that
we don't need to tell others about God. Tenderhearted in-
tellectuals say that everyone is entitled to his own belief;
therefore, there's no need for evangelism. So there has
been a sharp decline in missionary work. Major denominations are shutting down mission schools and hospitals;
they're now sending money to aid the "economic develop-
ment" of foreign nations.

In fact, the only Christian groups that have increased
their force of missionaries to the field these days are the
independent, evangelical churches, according to an article
in *Christianity Today*. We still believe God is supposed to
be worshipped by the entire world, not just white Anglo-
Saxon Protestants who make more than $30,000 a year.
In that article Harold Lindsell commented:

Many factors have contributed to the serious loss of
missionaries among the traditional ecumenical denominations. However...these figures are a rough
index of the depth of confliction about basic Christian doctrine—the nature of the gospel, the lostness

of mankind apart from Christ, and the necessity of obeying biblical mandates. [7]

We do have a mandate from God, a mandate to call the entire world to Him. Christ said, *"Go ye therefore, and teach all nations, baptizing them in the name of the Father, and of the Son, and of the Holy Ghost"* (Matthew 28:19). So our worship will never be complete until we tell others that the Lord is the one true God indeed, God in three persons, God of all the world, and worthy of our deepest devotion.

NOTES

1. Francis Brown, S. R. Driver, and Charles A. Briggs, eds., A Hebrew and English Lexicon of the Old Testament (Oxford: Oxford University Press, 1972), p. 43.

2. B. W Anderson, "God, Names of," *The Interpreter's Dictionary of the Bible,* Vol. 2 (Nashville: Abingdon Press, 1962), p. 413.

3. Samuel Sandmel, *The Hebrew Scriptures* (New York: Alfred A. Knopf, 1963), p. 329.

4. For more insight into how these nations ignored God, see my book, *Where Was God When Pagan Religions Began?* (Nashville: Thomas Nelson Publishers, 1980).

5. Fenelon, *Let Go* (New Kensington, Pa.: Whitaker House, 1973), p. 52.

6. A. W. Tozer, *The Best of A. W. Tozer,* ed. by Warren W. Wiersbe (Grand Rapids, Mich.: Baker Book House, 1978), pp. 189–190.

7. Harold Lindsell, "The Major Denominations Are Jumping Ship." *Christianity Today,* (September 18, 1981), p. 16.

Chapter 4

The Lord God Most High (Jehovah-Elyon)

Jehovah-Elyon should elicit praise upon praise from the fervent believer. This name for God is used about forty times in the Old Testament. It first appears in Genesis 14, in which King Melchizedek of Salem praises Abram's valiant rescue of his nephew Lot. Melchizedek said,

Blessed be Abram of the most high God, possessor of heaven and earth: and blessed be the most high God, which hath delivered thine enemies into thy hand.

(Genesis 14:19–20)

This name *Elyon* literally means "supreme God" or "most loved God." Notice why Melchizedek believes God is the "most high" and the "possessor of heaven and earth." He points out to Abram in verse 20 that God *"hath delivered thine enemies into thy hand."* And when you consider the frightful odds that Abram was up against—three hundred and eighteen household servants to fight the armies of the mightiest nations of that day (verses 1, 14)—you realize how great Abram's God had to be!

Pagan kings believed their gods helped them in battle. If they were defeated, they believed it was because their enemy's god was stronger than their own. So Melchizedek knew he spoke on good authority when he said Abram served "the Most High God," *Elyon.*

AN UNLIKELY VICTOR

To get a better idea of the magnitude of Abram's victory, notice that he had to pursue his enemies from the vicinity of Beersheba (in southern Canaan) to Dan, then divide his meager force of three hundred and eighteen men to keep on chasing the enemy by night to Damascus. (See Genesis 14:13–15.) Even today, if a tourist party in Beersheba wakes early in the morning and boards a bus or van for Damascus, it will be nightfall by the time they arrive. This was a long and perilous journey over rough terrain. Yet Abram made the trip. He pitted his tiny band of soldiers against larger armies. And he won! Surely he was serving "the Most High God."

Since Abram had also captured the war booty that his enemies had taken from Sodom and Gomorrah, the king of Sodom went out to meet Abram as he returned from battle. The king of Sodom offered Abram a deal. He said, *"Give me the persons* [i.e., the slaves], *and take the goods to thyself"* (verse 21). But Abram refused. He said,

> *I have lift up mine hand unto the LORD, the most high God [Jehovah-Elyon], the possessor of heaven and earth, That I will not take from a thread even to a shoelatchet, and that I will not take any thing that is thine, lest thou shouldest say, I have made Abram rich.* (Genesis 14:22–23)

Abram gave God all the credit for the victory he had won, and he would give God all the credit for the material blessings he would receive. When the day came that God would bless him with herds, land, and other kinds of wealth, Abram wanted no one to say, "I made Abram what he is today." So he gave the war booty back to the king of Sodom.

How about you? Is your life a "rags to riches" story?

How about you? Is your life a "rags to riches" story? If it is, to whom do you give the credit—to God or man? I have led some very wealthy businessmen to the Lord Jesus Christ; every one of them then started giving God the credit for their wealth. Before Jesus took over their lives, they boasted of their keen business sense and "lucky breaks"; but after Jesus took over, they gave God all the credit for their prosperity. That's the way it should be.

Abram gave God all the credit for his success. He wanted his ungodly neighbors to see how God blessed him; he wanted them to realize that he served "the Lord the Most High God."

A SELF-MADE MAN?

The attitude of Lot, Abram's nephew, was just the opposite of his uncle's. Lot kept trying to prove that he could make a successful life for himself, with no help from anyone else. He wanted to prove he could be a "self-made man."

When Uncle Abram let him choose his own portion of the land, Lot chose the best portion in hopes of making a great name for himself. The Bible says, *"Lot...pitched his tent toward Sodom. But the men of Sodom were wicked and sinners before the LORD exceedingly"* (Genesis 13:12–13). Lot chose to live in an area good for trading, despite the moral corruption that the "cities of the plain" might bring to his family.

Then Sodom and Gomorrah fell to their enemies, and Lot was carried off by the pagan armies of the East. Abram rescued him but turned over all the flocks and other possessions to the king of Sodom. So Lot lost everything he owned. At that point, the wisest thing Lot could have done would have been to say, "I see, Uncle Abram, that when

I'm with you, I'm on the winning side. When I'm with you, God blesses me. And when I try to make it on my own, I'm a slave."

But he didn't. He went right back to the city of Sodom, got a house for his family, and tried to eke out a living in that hellhole of corruption.

Soon God decided to destroy Sodom and Gomorrah, and He warned Lot to get out before it was too late. (See Genesis 19.) Lot took his family to the city of Zoar as God rained fiery brimstone upon Sodom and Gomorrah, scorching them from the face of the earth forever. You'll remember that Lot lost his wife in the process. When she disobeyed God and looked back at her hometown, God turned her into a pillar of salt.

> *After these cliff-hanger escapes, Lot should have known to trust Jehovah-Elyon to bless his life.*

You would think that by now Lot would have learned his lesson. After these cliff-hanger escapes, he should have known that he ought to trust *Jehovah-Elyon* to bless his life, instead of trying to bless himself.

But no, Lot soon decided to take his two daughters and retreat to a nearby mountain cave. Apparently, he intended to spend the rest of his life there as a hermit. What a classic portrait of human despair! When a man fails to succeed at his own plans for self-conceited success, all he wants is a lonely place to sulk. If he can't have the congratulations of others, he certainly doesn't want their pity. He would rather be forgotten. That's what Lot wanted to do: hide and be forgotten.

Do you see the contrast between Lot and his Uncle Abram? One man tried to make something of himself, the other let the Most High God make something of him. And which one succeeded?

Let's return to that conversation between Abram and Melchizedek, because it reveals two important facts about the Most High God. Look again at what Melchizedek said in Genesis 14:19: *"Blessed be Abram of the most high God, possessor of heaven and earth."* Because God is the Most High, He owns everything in creation. In fact, He created it to begin with! So it's easy to see how God can control every situation of our lives. He owns the universe. He's in charge of everything in it.

We once needed to build an important building for our ministry, and the state government required us to have two driveway exits. So the contractor approached the man who owned the adjacent property and asked to buy more of the property so we could meet the building code. The owner, however, did not want to sell.

Now this fellow was an elderly farmer. The ground we wanted to buy from him was open farmland. He would soon be dead, and the property would be of no use to him. But he would not sell. "They'll never get even a little bit of this land from me!" he said.

His attitude didn't bother me personally. I always say, "The Lord's will be done." We just didn't erect the building. But can you imagine the tragedy of thinking like that man! Why, none of us really own anything. When I die, my body will be put in a casket and buried six feet under; that's all the earthly "possession" that will be left to Lester Sumrall. I don't really own anything in this world. I'm just allowed to use some things for a little while, to bring glory to the Lord. He's the One who really owns it all.

> *I don't really own anything in this world. I'm just allowed to use some things for a little while.*

The Bible says that Abram *"gave him tithes of all"* (Genesis 14:20) because He realized God owned it all. He gave a tenth of the war spoils to this king-priest, as an offering to God, because he knew God really owned everything he had. This is the Bible's first reference to tithing and it comes at a most appropriate place in Scripture. We begin to tithe our money and other material goods to the Lord's work when we realize that the Most High God owns it all.

THE DELIVERER

Notice the second thing Melchizedek said about the Most High God: *"And blessed be the most high God, which hath delivered thine enemies into thy hand"* (Genesis 14:20). Not only does God own all things and all people, but he delivers them into the hands of His people.

Think about that for a moment: Did you realize that God will deliver your enemies into your hands? *Yes!!*

I think this is the thing most people don't understand about the ministry of deliverance. They know how much they would like to be delivered from sin, from illness, from demon possession, and so on. They want to escape from these things, and God offers them a way of escape. But there's another kind of deliverance that He promises, too. He promises to subdue certain problems His people experience.

God may not remove that malignant cancer from your body, but He will deliver the fear of cancer into your hands. He will give victory over the fear. God may not remove the hateful temper of your husband or wife, but He will deliver that temper into your hands. He will give you victory over it.

Hundreds of people have asked me to pray that God would deliver them from smoking, drinking, taking drugs,

* God subdued Donald Daneman on 5/4/09
Hallelujah to the God of gods!

and any number of other things. Yet they're surprised at how God delivers them. The cigarettes, booze, and drugs are still there; the temptation still faces them. But God gives them victory over the temptation. He delivers the enemies into their hands. Hallelujah!

Many people already have deliverance from their problems, but they don't claim it. Now what do I mean by that? I mean it's not enough to dream about deliverance from your problem. It's not enough to read your Bible and say, "My, look how God used to deliver people from this." You must claim God's promise to be *Jehovah-Elyon* in your life, and say, "I am delivered!" And you must keep on reminding yourself that God *has* delivered the enemy into your hand.

> *Many people already have deliverance from their problems, but they don't claim it.*

GOD IS GREATER, God is greatest

We may be so impressed by human achievements that we overlook the greatness of God Himself. You think I'm exaggerating, but it's true.

Many people have made a religion of modern technology; they think that scientists' ingenious minds can solve any problem that confronts them. They think they have no need for God; that, in fact, God only exists in the imagination of gullible people.

I'll agree that the human mind has achieved some marvelous things in recent years. Today I can leave New York or Washington on a magnificent supersonic plane and arrive in London less than three hours later. (The trip used to take nearly a month by boat.) I can sit down at a desktop computer, punch a few buttons, and call up thousands of facts about the stock market or medical science or any other area of interest to me. Those facts are stored on a plastic disc no bigger than a dinner plate. I can stand before a TV camera and preach a sermon, while my picture and the sound of my voice are instantaneously transmitted to millions of homes through a satellite hovering far above the earth. What a marvelous age in which to live!

But all of these marvels are just a taste of the infinite marvels God will reveal to us in eternity. God's mind is far greater than those He created. The Bible says, *"Eye hath not seen, nor ear heard, neither have entered into the heart of man, the things which God hath prepared for them that love him"* (1 Corinthians 2:9).

We Christians are going to live with God forever, in continuous awe of His majesty and glory. We will serve the Most High God throughout eternity. I'm so glad that the Most High God, *Jehovah-Elyon,* was not only Abram's God: He's the God of every born-again believer today.

God revealed Himself to Abram as *Jehovah-Elyon* in a moment of victory. At the moment of final victory, when Christ conquers Satan once and for all, the saints of God will certainly look heavenward and exclaim that He is greater than anyone else or any other power. He is truly the Most High God, *Jehovah-Elyon*.

CHAPTER 5

THE ALMIGHTY GOD
(EL-SHADDAI)

Genesis 17 tells how God appeared to Abram just after the birth of Ishmael, reminding him that they still had a covenant together. Abram was ninety-nine years old when this conversation began (verse 1), but he had turned one hundred by the time it ended (verse 17). So it must have been quite a prayer meeting! Notice what happened:

> *And when Abram was ninety years old and nine, the LORD appeared to Abram, and said unto him, I am the Almighty God [El-Shaddai]; walk before me, and be thou perfect. And I will make my covenant between me and thee, and will multiply thee exceedingly. And Abram fell on his face: and God talked with him.*
>
> (Genesis 17:1–3)

Here God reveals another of His names to the man that He promised would be the father of mighty nations.

God was teaching Abram more and more about Himself by giving him these different names for God. Each name had its own particular meaning, and revealed more of God's nature. The name "God Almighty," or *El-Shaddai* in the Hebrew, emphasizes God's ability to handle any situation that confronts His people. Dr. W. A. Criswell notes that *El-Shaddai*

> ...is a further enrichment of the supreme name YAHWEH. "El" is the singular form of *Elohim*, and "Shaddai" is literally "sufficient" or "self-sufficient"; therefore, it is rendered "almighty." The "almightiness" and "self-sufficiency" of YAHWEH are adequate for Him to deal victoriously and even destructively with His enemies.[1]

God wanted Abram to know He was in control of every situation. Abram might feel discouraged about trekking across the Near East to find the Promised Land; he might feel defeated by the prospect of fighting the strong warriors of Canaan to get the inheritance God had offered him. But God said there was no reason to feel discouraged and defeated. Abram just needed to remember that *El-Shaddai* would take care of him. The almighty God would not let his mission fail.

Satan wanted to destroy the nation of Israel even before it got started, so he threw all of his powers against Abram. The name Satan means "the Accuser," and Satan did his best to accuse Abram of failing. I can imagine Satan whispering into Abram's ear, "How can God make you a great nation? You have no children of your own, except for this boy you conceived in an illicit affair with your servant girl. You think God will use him to make a 'holy nation'? That's a laugh!"

Satan tries to destroy us from within, you see. He can give us physical trouble, and he can give us much opposition in the work we try to do for the Lord. But the front line for the battleground, as far as Satan is concerned, is your mind. He knows that if he can defeat your thoughts, he'll defeat your faith. He wants to make you skeptical of God's promises. So he seizes on every setback and problem as an accusation to bring to your mind; he begins whispering doubt in your ear. That's what he tried to do with Abram.

> The front line for the battleground, as far as Satan is concerned, is your mind.

But God told Abram, *"I am the Almighty God."* In other words, He said, "Abram, you see a lot of obstacles ahead. You see only the problems. But I'm bigger than any of your problems, and I'll fulfill My promises to you despite all the problems, if you'll turn them over to Me."

How many times God has had to remind me of that! I've been a minister of the gospel all my adult life, first as a foreign missionary and now as a pastor. Believe me, Satan works on nobody more than he works on a pastor or a missionary! He knows that if he can defeat God's leaders, he can defeat all of God's people.

So he works overtime at feeding doubts into my mind, and I've come close to being discouraged many times. But, praise God, the Almighty reminds me that He's able to take care of whatever trouble I'm facing! He may not show me *how* He's going to do it; He doesn't have to show me. He only reminds me that He is the almighty God, more powerful than any problem in my life. That's enough to lift the mist of defeat.

CONFESSING GOD'S POWER

So-called Christian psychologists often tell people to confess their weaknesses. Doing so allows you to be more human, they say. If you confess your weakness, you won't feel defeated so often because you'll know you're entitled to a few slip-ups.

The Bible does say that we are weak, humanly speaking. Paul admitted that Christians have the treasure of God's righteousness in *"earthen vessels"* (2 Corinthians 4:7)—clay pots that are liable to crack and break altogether. That's why we must rely on the Holy Spirit to give us God's own power every day. But if we concentrate on our weaknesses, rather than on the might of God, we set a limit on what God can do through us. Satan tried to make Abram believe he could never carry out God's plan because he was too old, too weak, and too travel-weary. But Abram stood his ground. He believed God. He may have looked weak, but his faith wasn't weak at all, and his God certain-ly wasn't weak. He was on God's side, and nobody is weak on God's side.

> Satan hopes you never find out that you're only as weak as you confess to be.

I'm not talking here about confessing sins. Certainly when we transgress God's law, we should confess and ask His forgiveness. (See 1 John 1:8–9.) I'm speaking here of lack of *faith*.

Here's something Satan hopes you never find out: *You're only as weak as you confess to be.* If you spend all your time talking about how weak you are, you set a puny human limit for the power of God. You've programmed yourself for failure. But the more you confess God's power, the more He can do for you.

Al Oerter was a track-and-field athlete who won the gold medal for discus throwing in the 1956 Olympics in Melbourne and the 1960 Olympics in Rome. He decided to try again at the 1964 Tokyo Olympics. His top competitor in Tokyo was a powerful Czech who had beat Al's old record just with his practice throws.

A week before the Olympics, Al tore the cartilage off the right side of his rib cage in a field practice accident. He had trouble with a cervical disc and had to wear a neck collar to keep it from hurting. Somehow he managed to qualify for the finals, but he had so much pain that his doctor advised him to drop out.

Don't make a fool of yourself, an inner voice whispered. *You've got an excuse. Withdraw!*

> Al trusted the Lord to provide the strength that he didn't have.

But Al Oerter suited up for the competition. He felt he had to try, in spite of the pain. When it came time for Al to throw the discus, he stepped into the ring and prayed, "God, give me strength."

His first toss was not particularly good, but it was good enough to get him into the last string of finalists. He had three more chances. His next throw was a failure, and the pain in his side and neck got worse.

But Al trusted the Lord to provide the strength he didn't have. He stepped back into the ring and threw the discus one more time. It sailed over 200 feet down the field for a new world record—and Al's third gold medal. Looking back on that day, Al said, "The important thing for all of us to remember is that wherever we want to go in life, we won't get there unless we bend all our efforts—mental, physical, and spiritual—toward that end."[2]

What do you do when you face a problem that's bigger than you can handle? Do you confess your weakness? Or do you confess God's power? You ought to do both. You ought to let God be "God Almighty" in your life.

HONORING AN ALMIGHTY GOD

If God is all-powerful and all-sufficient, and we are just *"earthen vessels,"* that raises another dilemma: How can we possibly have fellowship with Him? How can God tolerate us? God answered those questions for Abram when He said, *"Walk before me, and be thou perfect"* (Genesis 17:1).

God Almighty expects His people to live differently than everyone else. Many people today who think they know God go on living like the rest of the world. Women who claim to be God-fearing Christians still dress like Jezebel, prancing their endowments seductively before the eyes of men. But God wants us to know that we walk before Him. Our actions and thoughts are under the scrutiny of God Almighty, so they should not be like the actions and thoughts of carnal, unregenerate sinners. God's people can't live like Sodomites without being destroyed along with Sodom. (See Matthew 11:20–24.)

When God says, *"Be thou perfect,"* He is referring to moral perfection. He means we should live clean and godly lives before Him. Christian, don't sin against God and try to excuse yourself by saying, "Oh well, I'm only human." You're redeemed! You're a child of God! You are in union with Jesus Christ. Look like it, walk like it, talk like it, and live like it. That's the only way you can honor the almighty God you serve, and it's the only way He will continue to have fellowship with you.

Christian businessman J. Daniel Hess writes:

God is the Creator, the Definer of the good, the Maker of reality, the Head of the divine kingdom. All of our work and each of our obligations are subjected to the claims of God's creation and God's kingdom. To fulfill those obligations, we become servants of Christ.[3]

In other words, the only way we can fulfill God's design for our lives is to obey Him. That's true on the job, at home, in the school board meeting, riding a plane—wherever you are. God expects you to "walk before Him, and be perfect."

God blesses people who "walk before Him" in moral purity. The second time Jacob and his sons needed grain from Egypt, Jacob sent them there with twice as much money as they had been charged before, plus the money they had found in their bags, which they thought was *"an* oversight" (Genesis 43:12). And Jacob said, *"God Almighty [El-Shaddai] give you mercy before the man, that he may send away your other brother, and Benjamin"* (Genesis 43:14). He believed that if his sons did what was right, God the Almighty would bless them.

When Jacob called his sons to his deathbed for a final blessing he said to Joseph, *"The archers have sorely grieved him, and shot at him, and hated him: but his bow abode in strength, and the arms of his hands were made strong by the hands of the mighty God of Jacob...Even by the God of thy father, who shall help thee; and by the Almighty [Shaddai], who shall bless thee"* (Genesis 49:23–25). Jacob knew God would bless Joseph because the young man had done what was right, regardless of what his brothers had done to him. God the Almighty honors those who honor Him with a holy life.

> *God the Almighty honors those who honor Him with a holy life.*

Notice that God first told Abram to "be perfect," *then* He will "make a covenant" with us; if we don't, He offers us nothing.

There's no telling what wonderful things God would do in our lives if we started doing all that He tells us to do. The moment we question God, however, we blunt His blessings. When God gives us an order and promises to bless us if we carry out that order, we shouldn't say, "Now wait a minute, Lord. Just how are You going to do this?" The person of faith must walk in simple confidence that the Lord will do what He has said He will do.

One night as I prayed to the Lord, He told me that He wanted me to win a million souls for Him. Imagine that! Why, I would have been thrilled to win even a hundred souls for the Lord—but a million! Yet when God says that He's going to do a certain thing, we'd better believe Him. And I believe He's going to bless my ministry in just that way, if I keep on obeying Him.

GOD—THE BEGINNING OF GREATNESS

I'm sure that if Abraham told his neighbors what God had promised to do for him, they would have thought he was crazy. A great nation would come of this wizened old tent-dweller? This century-old codger would have more sons by his ninety-year-old wife? I'm sure Abraham's friends would have laughed at the very thought; it would have seemed so preposterous, so impossible.

But God needs men and women who are willing to be considered crazy for His sake. The Lord needs Christians who will stand up with Paul and say, *"We are fools for Christ's sake, but ye are wise in Christ"* (1 Corinthians 4:10). The only way this world will learn the truth of the gospel is if people like you and I will "stick our necks out" to believe what God promises.

That's what Abraham did. (God gave him a new name.) At first he, too, thought God's promise was laughable; but he went right ahead and believed it. Sarah, his wife, said, *"God hath made me to laugh, so that all that hear will laugh with me"* (Genesis 21:6). And she said, *"Who would have said unto Abraham, that Sarah should have given children suck? for I have born him a son in his old age"* (verse 7). Only God could have promised them such a thing. Anyone else would have found it impossible to fulfill such a promise, but *"with God all things are possible"* (Matthew 19:26).

> *At first Abraham thought God's promise was laughable; but he believed it.*

If I had told the people of my congregation twenty years ago what God would do with our radio and TV ministry, they would have burst out laughing. Who could have believed that He would give us the ownership of eight TV stations, plus a radio station? Who would have believed that we would make hundreds of audiocassettes and videocassettes of our worship services each week to send to people around the world? Who would have believed that our basement would be jammed full of printing presses, mailing machines, and complex electronic gear? Who would have believed that we would operate our own Christian college, which sends missionaries around the globe? Nobody would have believed it. But all these things have come to pass by the grace of the Lord. We had better believe Jesus when He says, *"With God all things are possible."*

The prophet Isaiah predicted that God would send His Anointed One to deliver the nation of Israel from all their enemies, especially the spiritual enemy of Satan. But Isaiah also said, *"Who hath believed our report? and to whom is the arm of the LORD revealed?"* (Isaiah 53:1). The answer was simple—only the ones who had courage enough to believe that God does what He says He will do. Believers may be accounted fools, as far as the world is concerned, but they are wise in the eyes of the Lord. They are the ones who will see *"the arm of the LORD revealed"* in mighty and wondrous works.

When I was a boy, we had lots of wall mottoes hanging in our home. Each one had a Bible verse or some other statement designed to strengthen our faith. And one of those wall mottoes said, "I am the El-Shaddai." If a visitor didn't know what that meant, my mother could take an hour to tell him. I still remember how excited she would become as she told how great, how wonderful, and how powerful God really is.

My friend, you and I need to rejoice in God's greatness today. We need to remind ourselves that He is indeed

El-Shaddai, "God the Almighty," and that He can handle any problem that faces us. It's so easy to have puny faith because we assume God is puny. We secretly think He's not able to make much difference in our lives. But when we realize that He is the almighty God, the all-powerful Ruler of the Universe, we begin to see wonderful things happen in our lives. Our faith becomes great as we realize God is great.

Dr. Robert H. Schuller tells of a tourist who walked down a seaside pier one afternoon and saw a fisherman pull in a big fish, measure it, and throw it back in the ocean. This intrigued the tourist, so he kept watching. Soon the fisherman caught a much smaller fish, measured

> *Our faith becomes great as we realize God is great.*

it, and dropped it in his bucket. He kept doing this for some time—throwing the big fish back, keeping the little fish. So the tourist asked him why he did this.

"Why," the fisherman said, "because my frying pan is only ten inches across!"[4]

Are you doing that with God's promises? Are you "throwing back" the overwhelming miracles that He wants to do in your life, and "keeping" only the small, believable things that He promises? Let God be *El-Shaddai* in your life! Let Him be the almighty God that He can be! Put your trust in His infinite greatness, and He'll make you what He wants you to be!

Pay careful attention to what God promised Abraham in Genesis 17:8:

> *And I will give unto thee, and to thy seed after thee, the land wherein thou art a stranger, all the land of Canaan, for **an everlasting possession**; and I will be their God.*　　　　　　　(emphasis added)

God granted Abraham the entire land of Canaan as an everlasting possession for him and his family. The Jews have been evicted from that land time and again, but they always come back because it belongs to them. *God honored Abraham's faith by giving him the only permanent real estate grant on the face of the earth.* That's how great God is!

The diplomats of the United Nations have bent all their human wisdom to solving the problem of dividing up the land of Palestine. They're not sure how much land should go to Israel, how much to Jordan, how much to Egypt, and how much to the Palestine Liberation Front. But there's only one problem with all their debating and political maneuvering! God says the land will always belong to Israel. I don't say that because I'm pro-Israel or anti-Palestinian; I say that because the Word of God says it. God is great enough to back up His promise to Abraham, and He will do so long after the United Nations has disbanded. And He will make His promise stick, because He is *El-Shaddai*.

God gave Abraham two sons, Ishmael and Isaac. Ishmael was the ancestor of the Arab people, while Isaac was the ancestor of the Jews. These two groups of people account for much of the material wealth in our world today. I'm not saying this to draw attention to the Jews or Arabs, but to draw attention to the One who made them what they are. God the Almighty has not failed in His promise to the descendants of Ishmael and Isaac, even today. And He's going to keep His promises for all eternity.

> *God blesses the people who believe He is as great as He really is.*

God blesses the people who believe He is as great as He really is. God even blesses the children of people who believe.

I know liberal theologians would deny the above statement; nevertheless it's true. It would be interesting to make a study of the top officers of the "Fortune 500" companies, and see how many of them are the sons and daughters of devout, godly parents. I think you'd find a surprisingly large number of them are. (I'm acquainted with some of these people, so I know my statement is not just a "shot in the dark.") Make a survey of the members of Congress, the governors of our states, and the other top political leaders of our nation, and I think you'll find that most of them grew up in God-fearing, God-honoring homes. I have talked with some of the chief political leaders of our land, and most of them say that their parents prayed for them. Their parents said, "Lord, I claim Your promises. Bless my children." And the Lord did.

So no matter how simplistic it may sound, I repeat it to you: *God blesses people who believe He is as great as He really is. Furthermore, He blesses their children. "For He remembered His holy promise, And Abraham His servant. He brought out His people with joy, His chosen ones with gladness"* (Psalm 105:42–43 NKJV).

OBEY HIS WORD—CLAIM HIS POWER

Of course, these promises didn't just fall into the lap of Abraham's children. They had to stay true to God's covenant with Abraham before He could bless them as He desired. *"And God said unto Abraham, Thou shalt keep my covenant therefore, thou, and thy seed after thee in their generations. This is my covenant, which ye shall keep, between me and you and thy seed after thee"* (Genesis 17:9–10).

"Brother Sumrall," you say, "do you expect me to believe that all the Jews have obeyed God's covenant?" Of course not. In fact, history proves that most of the Jews rejected God's covenant and denied His own beloved Son who came to die for them. But a few were faithful, and God kept blessing the nation because of them. When God predicted the doom of Israel at the hands of the marauding Assyrians and Babylonians, He said,

I will also leave in the midst of thee an afflicted and poor people, and they shall trust in the name of the LORD. The remnant of Israel shall not do iniquity, nor speak lies; neither shall a deceitful tongue be found in their mouth: for they shall feed and lie down, and none shall make them afraid. (Zephaniah 3:12–13)

This faithful remnant of the Jews kept God's covenant alive. They were the reason God continued to bless the Jews, even when the majority of them turned away from Him. Their enemies would triumph over them for a time, but in the end *"the residue of my people shall spoil them, and the remnant of my people shall possess them"* (Zephaniah 2:9). Though most Jews disobeyed God and disregarded His covenant, enough were loyal to keep open the channel to His covenant blessings. Today there are thousands of Jewish Christians—Jews who have accepted Jesus as their Messiah—living in the land of Israel. They are living by God's New Covenant, sealed with the blood of Christ. We can expect God to keep on blessing Israel materially because of their faithfulness.

And what about the descendants of Ishmael? How do we account for the tremendous power that the Arabs have today?

Again, we must trace it back to a faithful remnant who have kept Abraham's covenant with God. Granted, they are the "black sheep" of the covenantal family because of Ishmael's illegitimate descent from Abraham. Nevertheless, they belong to that family. Though they are not saved, the fact that God is blessing them indicates that some of them must still be faithful to Him. Bible scholar Dr. William Smith notes:

> *The fact that God is blessing them indicates that some must still be faithful to Him.*

The sons of Ishmael peopled the north and west of the Arabian penninsula, and eventually formed the chief element of the Arab nation, the wandering Bedoin tribes. They are now mostly Mohammedans, who look to him [i.e., Mohammed] as their spiritual father, as the Jews look to Abraham.[5]

But remember that Mohammed was not born until the sixth century A.D. What happened to Ishmael's descendants until that time? Many became Christians! In fact, Mohammed had to convert several Christian communities in Arabia before he could consolidate his power there.[6] Mohammed had so many Christian friends that his Islamic doctrine was actually "a theology which partook of elements of Judaism, Christianity, and Arabian heathenism."[7] Many of Ishmael's descendants were won to Christ during the six hundred years before Mohammed's fanatical campaign.

Mohammed tried to wipe out Christianity in Arabia, but he failed. There are still a few small, strong, tenacious Christian communities in Egypt, Iran, Saudi Arabia, and the other oil-rich Arab nations of the Middle East. Is it really a coincidence, then, that God has blessed these nations? I think not. *Egypt is not blessed, but very poor*

God the Almighty, *El-Shaddai,* is far greater than any political theory or economic system or social utopia. God blesses those who are faithful to Him, even when His blessing contradicts human logic. And in the case of the Jews and Arabs, we see God blessing the descendants of one man who, by all human odds, would have been long forgotten in the dust of history except for one thing, *"Abraham believed God, and it was accounted to him for righteousness"* (James 2:23 NKJV).

Do you believe God is almighty? Do you believe God will give you *"every good and perfect gift"* that you need to serve Him (James 1:17)? Then be ready for God to do some marvelous things in your life and in the lives of your children.

NOTES

1. W. A. Criswell, ed., *The Criswell Study Bible* (Nashville: Thomas Nelson Publishers, 1979), p. 27.

2. Al Oerter, "The Challenge," *Guideposts* (April 1980), p. 5.

3. J. Daniel Hess, *Ethics in Business and Labor* (Scottdale, Pa.: Herald Press, 1977), p. 64.

4. Robert H. Schuller, *You Can Become the Person You Want to Be* (Old Tappan, N.J.: Spire Books, 1976), p. 21.

5. William Smith, *A Dictionary of the Bible,* ed. and Revelation by E. N. and M. A. Peloubet (Nashville: Thomas Nelson Publishers, 1979), p. 269.

6. William M. Miller, *A Christian's Response to Islam* (Wheaton, Ill.: Tyndale House Publishers, Inc., 1980), p. 35.

7. Howard F. Vos, *Highlights of Church History* (Chicago: Moody Press, 1960), p. 53.

CHAPTER 6

THE LORD WILL PROVIDE (JEHOVAH-JIREH)

In the hour when Abraham's faith was tested more severely, God revealed another of His names. This name encouraged Abraham's faith and should encourage our faith today. The name is *Jehovah-Jireh,* which means "the LORD will provide."

Turn to Genesis 21:33 to pick up the story of Abraham.

> *And Abraham planted a grove in Beersheba, and called there on the name of the LORD, the everlasting God. And Abraham sojourned in the Philistines' land many days. And it came to pass after these things, that God did tempt Abraham.* (Genesis 21:33–22:1)

The word *tempt* is not a very good rendering of what the Hebrew manuscript says here. Other versions say that God *"tested"* Abraham (RSV, NASB, TLB). God never tempts a person to sin.

And [God] said unto him, Abraham: and he said, Behold, here I am. And he said, Take now thy son, thine only son Isaac, whom thou lovest, and get thee into the land of Moriah; and offer him there for a burnt offering upon one of the mountains which I will tell thee of.   (Genesis 22:1–2)

The region of Moriah is where Jerusalem is now located. At least seven hills, or "mounts," form the citadel of the city.

> God provided a specific place for Abraham to worship Him.

I well remember visiting Jerusalem with a tour guide some years ago. He said to me, "Isn't it interesting that Abraham found the right hill for his sacrifice? Because if he hadn't, he would have found no ram there" (compare Genesis 22:13). God had one ram prepared for Abraham, and one hill where He wanted Abraham to offer his sacrifice. Abraham didn't know he'd found the right hill until he had gotten there. Aren't you glad that God is wiser than we are?

God provided a specific place for Abraham to worship Him. I believe God still does that for His people. I believe certain people are supposed to be worshipping in the Christian Center, where I am pastor; when they worship elsewhere, they don't get the blessing they would have received at the Center. Likewise I know some people have tried worshipping in my congregation who should have been worshipping elsewhere. Sometimes I've had to tell them so. They didn't realize what a blessing they missed until they worshipped with the people God intended them to worship with, and in the way He intended them to worship. God's plans for us are that specific.

> *And Abraham rose up early in the morning, and saddled his ass, and took two of his young men with him, and Isaac his son, and clave the wood for the burnt offering, and rose up, and went unto the place of which God had told him.* (Genesis 22:3)

Abraham was ready to obey the Lord. He didn't say, "Now listen, Lord, it will take me a few days to get things ready." God told him what to do, and the very next morning Abraham set out to do it.

If you study the lives of other spiritual giants, you will find they were like Abraham in this respect. They never hesitated to do what God told them. They never consulted with their friends before deciding whether to obey the Lord. Suppose Abraham had called his oldest servant and said, "Eleazar, you're my chief counselor here. Someday I'm planning to send you to find a wife for my son Isaac. But the Lord says I should take Isaac over into Moriah and burn him on an altar there. What do you think I should do?"

The servant probably would have said, "Well! If you do what you think the Lord's told you to do, we won't have anyone to find a wife for! Have you gone crazy?"

Friend, if you depend only on other people to tell you God's will for your life, you will miss His will every time. As long as you keep tugging at your friend's shirttail saying, "What do you think I should do?" you make it that much harder for God to speak to you.

I believe the Holy Spirit guides us both from within and from without, in a marvelous way. He does not have

> *I believe the Holy Spirit guides us both from within and from without, in a marvelous way.*

to knock us down with thunderbolts to get God's message across; He just indicates the direction in which we should go, and the open doors we should follow. Then He leaves the rest to us. (That is not to say that we are to neglect the wise counsel of more mature Christians, such as our elders. Hebrews 13:17 says to *"obey them that have the rule over you* [spiritually], *and submit yourselves: for they watch for your souls."*)

I believe that every child of God is living in the will of God, unless he or she has rebelled against it consciously. I don't believe the will of God is some dark, unfathomable secret that requires you to weep and scream in order to find it. As long as you are obeying the inner direction of His Spirit and have the inner peace that He gives to His obedient children, you don't need to consult every Tom, Dick, and Harry before you decide to act.

I have seen this in my own experience as a father. A father can't follow his children everywhere they go; if he tried, he would wear himself out. He must trust them to obey him even when he's out of sight. Only when his children rebel openly against his will or ignore his will does the father need to discipline them.

Always remember that God is your loving Father. He doesn't hound you with His will; He simply reveals His will to you, then trusts you to follow it. And the only time you'll feel His chastening hand of punishment is when you violate or ignore His will.

Notice what Abraham did next:

Then on the third day Abraham lifted up his eyes, and saw the place afar off. And Abraham said unto his young men, Abide ye here with the ass; and I and the lad will go yonder and worship, and come again to you. (Genesis 22:4–5)

The journey from Beersheba to Moriah was long and difficult. No wonder Abraham took two servant boys with him! But when they arrived at the place of worship, he left the servants with his donkey. God had commanded that the sacrifice be offered by him and his son alone. Yet he confidently said that they would *"come again"* to the servants. Now what did he mean by that? He meant that he believed his son would live, no matter what happened on top of that rocky hill. I can imagine him saying, "Lord, even if my son goes up in flames, I'll command those ashes to stand up straight and walk back down the hill with me." That was faith! Abraham knew God had promised him a son—in fact, had promised a long line of descendants to him—so he knew his son would live.

> *And Abraham took the wood of the burnt offering, and laid it upon Isaac his son; and he took the fire in his hand, and a knife; and they went both of them together. And Isaac spake unto Abraham his father, and said, My father: and he said, Here am I, my son. And he said, Behold the fire and the wood: but where is the lamb for a burnt offering? And Abraham said, My son, God will provide [Jehovah-Jireh] himself a lamb for a burnt offering: so they went both of them together.* (Genesis 22:6–8)

What an amazing exhibition of faith! With a knife in his hand and the flames billowing from his torch, he told his son, *"God will provide himself a lamb for a burnt offering."*

And they came to the place which God had told him

of; and Abraham built an altar there, and laid the
wood in order, and bound Isaac his son, and laid
him on the altar upon the wood.   (Genesis 22:9)

At this point, Abraham's faith had to become Isaac's
faith as well. The old man
had promised that God would
provide a sacrifice, and now
he laid his own son upon the
sacrificial trough. I imagine
he must have whispered in
Isaac's ear, "Don't be afraid,
Son. Go with me all the way
and don't be afraid. And if
you feel a little frightened,
just close your eyes and think of Jehovah."

> At this point, Abraham's faith had to become Isaac's faith as well.

And Abraham stretched forth his hand, and took the
knife to slay his son. And the angel of the LORD called
unto him out of heaven, and said, Abraham, Abra-
ham: and he said, Here am I. And he said, Lay not
thine hand upon the lad, neither do thou any thing
unto him: for now I know that thou fearest God,
seeing thou hast not withheld thy son, thine only son
from me.   (Genesis 22:10–12)

God's messenger brought a stay of execution at the last
possible moment. Abraham's faith was tested to capacity,

and proved strong. God regarded that faith by sparing his son Isaac.

> *And Abraham lifted up his eyes, and looked, and behold behind him a ram caught in a thicket by his horns: and Abraham went and took the ram, and offered him up for a burnt offering in the stead of his son. And Abraham called the name of that place Jehovahjireh.* (Genesis 22:13–14)

Today the Mosque of Omar stands on the spot where Abraham is said to have made this historic sacrifice. Under the dome of that mosque is a massive stone, the Stone of Abraham, with a large cave at the base of it. Tradition says that King Solomon offered animal sacrifices here, letting the blood flow down into the cave. We do not know whether that is true, but we do know that when Abraham and Isaac stood on that spot, there were no buildings there. Nothing obstructed their view of the seven hills of Moriah. They could see the hill of Golgotha, just a few hundred feet away, where Jesus Christ would offer His life as the final and complete sacrifice for man's sins. Jesus would tell the Jews, *"Your father Abraham rejoiced to see my day: and he saw it, and was glad"* (John 8:56).

Oh, what a day of rejoicing that must have been! How jubilant Abraham and Isaac must have been as they raised their hands heavenward and exclaimed, *"Jehovah-Jireh: The LORD will provide!"*

110

X The Beast is to come out of a city w/ 7 Hills
Everyone thinks of Rome, but as the wicked one
is an imitator, why not Jerusalem? 6/14/2011 CW

Not only was *Jehovah-Jireh* their name for that place; we might say it was their name for God. For at that moment they knew God was the Provider of all they needed. He had provided the Lamb that all mankind would need for sacrifice. *Jehovah-Jireh:* "The LORD will provide!"

HIS PROVISION FOR YOU

When soldiers march into battle, they carry provisions in their knapsacks—food, water, and vitamins—to give their bodies strength for the conflict.

Whether or not you realize it, God gives you provisions for the spiritual battles you face. When you surrender your life to Christ and let Him take full control, you become a soldier in the Lord's army. As the famed missionary Hudson Taylor once said, "God's work done in God's way cannot fail to have God's provision."

On the very night He was betrayed, Jesus asked His disciples, *"When I sent you without purse, and scrip, and shoes, lacked ye any thing? And they said, Nothing"* (Luke 22:35). God provided the food, clothing, and money that these first evangelists needed when they set out to tell the world about Jesus. The same is true today. God provides what His servants need to serve Him.

I am a living testimony to that fact. Everything that I have today came from the Lord's hand. In fact, I owe my very life to Him, because I have been on the brink of death twice and He has cured me miraculously. In each instance I found that when I committed myself to serve Him with every fiber of my being, He gave me the health and strength to survive.

Today some people drive past our property in South Bend and say, "My, doesn't Brother Sumrall have a beautiful house?" That's true, but it reflects no credit on Lester Sumrall; all the credit goes to the Lord, who provided that house for me. Some people walk through our television studios at South Bend or Indianapolis and exclaim, "Well, Brother Sumrall has certainly spared no expense here!" I agree: it's expensive to do a first-class job of television ministry. Our equipment, however, is no credit to me; it's a credit to the Lord who provided it.

> The Lord will provide everything a Christian needs to tell unsaved friends about Jesus.

The Lord will provide everything a Christian needs to tell unsaved friends about Jesus. Whether it's something material or spiritual, obvious or hidden—the right book to loan or true insight into what that one needs to hear—regardless of what is needed, the Lord will provide it, as long as you use His provision to service Him.

And God is able to make all grace abound toward you; that ye, always having all sufficiency in all

*things, may abound to every good work: (As it is
written, He hath dispersed abroad; he hath given to
the poor: his righteousness remaineth for ever. Now
he that ministereth seed to the sower both minister
bread for your food, and multiply your seed sown,
and increase the fruits of your righteousness).*

(2 Corinthians 9:8–10)

Notice the promise that God gives us in those three
short verses of Scripture:

God will "minister seed to the sower." When you commit yourself to be a witness for the Lord, He will give you
a message to share. If you're the wife of an unsaved man,
God will show you how to tell your mate about Jesus. If
you're a Christian teacher in the public schools, God will
show you how to be a shining witness in the classroom. If
you're a young preacher in your first pastorate, God will
give you those sermon outlines and open the Scriptures to
your understanding. No matter where you plan to "sow"
the gospel, you can be sure that God will give you the
"seed."

God will "minister bread for your food." This is the
kind of provision Hudson Taylor was talking about, and
the kind I have experienced myself. The psalmist said, *"I
have been young, and now am old; yet have I not seen the
righteous forsaken, nor his seed begging bread"* (Psalm
37:25). That was true long before the days of food stamps
and Social Security; it's still true today. God doesn't let

His people go hungry. He doesn't let them wear ragged tatters for clothes. He doesn't abandon them to die of exposure in the snow. God provides for the physical needs of His children.[1]

God will *"multiply your seed sown."* In other words, God will take care of convicting the hearts of unsaved people that hear the gospel from you. Don't feel discouraged if your unsaved friends don't clamor to become Christians. Your job is to tell them about Jesus. Then God's Holy Spirit can begin His convicting work in their lives. (See John 16:8–11.) He will bring fruit from the seed that you sow.

> *God will take care of convicting the hearts of unsaved people that hear the gospel from you.*

God will *"increase the fruits of your righteousness."* He promises not only to multiply the fruit of your witnessing, but the fruit of your very way of living. James 3:18 says, *"The fruit of righteousness is sown in peace of them that make peace."* And Galatians 5:22–23, 25 says, *"But the fruit of the Spirit is love, joy, peace, longsuffering, gentleness, goodness, faith, meekness, temperance: against such there is no law...If we live in the Spirit, let us also walk in the Spirit."* The fruit of righteousness, then, is the outward manifestation of being filled with God's Holy Spirit.

One who is so filled evidences all of the godly attitudes described above. God will cause these attitudes to emerge in your life as you serve Him.

These are God's provisions for you if you are one of His children. You can enjoy these provisions only if you are His child. And how do you become His child? Jesus explained that to the Jewish leader Nicodemus, saying:

> *Except a man be born of water and of the Spirit, he cannot enter into the kingdom of God. That which is born of the flesh is flesh; and that which is born of the Spirit is spirit. Marvel not that I said unto thee, Ye must be born again.* (John 3:5–7)

That's how you get these precious provisions of God— by being "born again" through the cleansing water of salvation and the empowering Spirit of Christ. You must repent of your sins, claim Jesus as your only Savior, and let Him fill you with His Holy Spirit. When you join the ranks of the reborn, you inherit all the precious provisions of God.

God also provides for us in the midst of trouble. Billy Graham has said:

> I seriously doubt if we will ever understand our trials and adversities until we are safely in heaven. Then when we look back we are going to be absolutely amazed at how God took care of us and blessed us

even in the storms of life. We face dangers every day of which we are not even aware.[2]

Yes, God will provide the help we need to live our lives for Him. He will provide the patience to endure hardships for His sake. And finally, He will provide an eternal home for us around His heavenly throne. *Jehovah-Jireh:* The LORD will provide!

NOTES

1. Someone naturally asks, "What about the Christians in East Africa who are starving to death? Or the Christians in India and the Caribbean who have no homes? Doesn't God provide for them?" I would say, Yes. God does provide for them, but the people who are in a position to deliver the goods in His name do not always follow His instructions. I'm afraid that many of us Americans are sitting on top of God's provision for our Christian brothers and sisters in those other countries and refusing to share that provision as we should. God will hold us responsible.

2. Billy Graham, *Till Armageddon: A Perspective on Suffering* (Waco, Tex.: Word Books, 1981), p. 168.

CHAPTER 7

THE LORD IS HEALER
(JEHOVAH-REPHEKA)

God made our bodies, and God is able to heal them and keep them healthy when we meet His conditions by obeying His instructions. God demonstrated this to the children of Israel as Moses led them out of bondage in Egypt.

Exodus chapter 15 tells how the Israelites rejoiced to see God deliver them from the Egyptians. You'll remember that God parted the Red Sea so they could cross over on dry ground, then He let the waters come flooding in upon the pursuing Egyptian hordes. What a day of victory that was! And the Israelites celebrated with singing and dancing, with Moses' sister Miriam leading the festivities. (See Exodus 15:20–21.) But three days later, when they were unable to find good drinking water, the Israelites started grumbling. (See verses 22–24.)

Isn't that just like fickle human nature? We forget God's goodness so easily. But in this moment of distress,

God spoke to His people through Moses and revealed another name for Himself, a name that would encourage them for years to come:

> *There he made for them a statute and an ordinance, and there he proved them, and said, If thou wilt diligently hearken to the voice of the LORD thy God, and wilt do that which is right in his sight, and wilt give ear to his commandments, and keep all his statutes, I will put none of these diseases upon thee, which I have brought upon the Egyptians: for I am the LORD that healeth thee [Jehovah-Repheka].* (Exodus 15:25–26)

Notice that God said, "I am the Lord who heals you *if* you'll do what I've told you to do." His promise came with a requirement, a condition that the Israelites had to meet if they wanted Him to heal them.

THE "WHY?" QUESTION

Many people come to my study and ask such questions as these: "Brother Sumrall, why haven't I been healed?" "Why did my mother die?" "Why was my baby born handicapped?"

We all have a lot of "why?" questions. I have plenty of my own. Not all of them will be answered in this life. They will have to wait until we join the Lord in heaven. But Exodus 15:26 gives some insight into many of the questions we have about healing.

So many of our "why" questions would be answered if we only looked at the way we live, and compared it with the standard of living required by the Word of God. Then we would realize that we are not living up to God's conditions.

Most people read the *benefits* promised in God's Word, but they fail to read the *conditions* attached to them. And that's usually the reason they can't figure out why no healing has come.

> Most people read the benefits promised in God's Word, but fail to read the conditions.

If an insurance salesman comes to your house and offers you a policy for a million dollars, he won't start his sales pitch by telling you how much you'll have to pay to get such coverage. He'll start by selling you on how much you'll get from it. That's his job. He will say, "If you ever get sick, we'll pay you so much money every day; we'll take care of all your hospital bills; we'll pay the doctor everything you owe. If you get laid off work, we'll pay you so much workman's compensation." And so on and so on. Only when you get excited enough to "sign on the dotted line" will he tell you about the premiums you have to pay. He knows you'd much rather think about the benefits.

That's what the children of Israel were doing. They must have thought, "Isn't it fantastic to have all these benefits that the Lord is going to give us?" But they would pay no attention to the requirements He gave them; they would rather not think about doing *"that which is right in his sight,"* or *"giving ear to all his commandments,"* or *"keeping all his statutes."*

We are the same way, of course. We are so eager to get God's benefits that we forget what He requires of us. So we go a couple of steps forward in our Christian life, then slide back a step. We get saved and start testifying like a zealot, then fizzle when the first bit of trouble comes along. If we would just stick to the Word of God and obey what He tells us to do in it, God would bless us.

God intended for all His children to be healthy. Adam and Eve were created perfect, without ailments. Even though we rejected God's goodness and rejected the health He offers (through the Fall), He was merciful and gave us healing instead.

Someone is bound to say, "What about the faithful Christians who keep on suffering? What about people who are serving the Lord with all their hearts, but still don't get healed?"

People like Joni Eareckson-Tada have struggled with this question deeply. A diving accident left her paralyzed, changing her life dramatically. Her only answer is that

God knows what He is doing. She is being made Christlike, and God is being glorified in her infirmities, more than He would be glorified in her physical healing. The same was true for Paul. (See 2 Corinthians 12:7–9.) We may not fully understand how this is to our benefit or how God can be glorified in this way, but He is. There are special cases in which God demonstrates His love through giving patience and strength instead of healing. God wants His people to be healthy—spiritually and physically. So sometimes He is healing (perfecting) our spiritual lives first. He wants His ailing people to be healed. The overarching will of God is to heal us of all our diseases, that He may be glorified by our healing.

LOOKING TO CHRIST

Numbers 21 describes a situation in which God proved His healing mercy to the children of Israel. They had been wandering in the wilderness for a long time without getting into the Promised Land, and they started to grumble again. They said to Moses, *"Wherefore have ye brought us up out of Egypt to die in the wilderness? for there is no bread, neither is there any water; and our soul loatheth this light bread"* (Numbers 21:5).

God was giving them manna from heaven. In their rebelliousness, however, they said, "We don't care for it." They were saying, "Thanks for the meat, Lord, but we want filet mignon." They forgot that God was supplying their needs; they started complaining and begging for some of their wants.

So the Lord allowed fiery serpents to attack their camp. Many Israelites were bitten and died. Suddenly the survivors realized how well-off they had been before. They came to Moses and said, *"We have sinned, for we have spoken against the LORD, and against thee"* (Numbers 21:7).

> *They forgot that God was supplying their needs; they started complaining and begging for their wants.*

So Moses prayed for the people. The Lord instructed him to make a serpent of brass and set it upon a pole in the midst of their camp, promising that anyone who was bitten by a snake could look upon that snake and live. The Lord would heal the victims of the snakebites.

The notes to the Scofield Bible indicate that the serpents represented sin, while brass represented divine judgment (as in the brazen altar). Therefore, according to Scofield, the brass serpent represented Christ—God who became sin on our behalf. Jesus Himself pointed out this connection when He said to Nicodemus:

And as Moses lifted up the serpent in the wilderness, even so must the Son of man be lifted up:

that whosoever believeth in him should not perish, but have eternal life. (John 3:14–15)

The Israelites were to look at the brass serpent and receive healing; we are to look unto Christ and receive healing. All of our healing—physical or spiritual—comes from the Lord.

It's so hard to get people to understand this. They travel all over the country to faith-healing services; they listen to tapes about healing; they buy all the latest books about healing; they take herb cures and every other kind of treatment that promises healing. But there is no healing virtue in these things. There is no healing virtue in an evangelist, in a church, or in a theory of any kind. There is healing virtue only in Christ; only He was made sin for us. Sin is the cause of all our suffering. Sometimes suffering comes to us because of Adam's sin; sometimes it comes because of some more immediate transgression. But sin is always the cause of suffering. And Christ took all of our sins to the cross. He suffered in our place, so that *"with his stripes we are healed"* (Isaiah 53:5).

Jesus said, *"And I, if I be lifted up from the earth, will draw all men unto me"* (John 12:32). Maybe church attendance is sluggish because people seldom see Jesus lifted up in our churches. We read in the newspapers that a congregation is about to launch a two-million-dollar building program, or that a certain preacher has just started a new series of prophecy lectures, or that a musical group is about to have a spectacular concert. But we seldom see Jesus lifted up. We seldom hear testimonies of how He has cast demons out of someone. We seldom hear about other ways He has worked in people's lives. Is it any wonder, then, that people are so indifferent to the church?

God's Word is true. God does heal people today. God does save sinful souls today. God does cast out evil spirits today. I know He does because I see Him doing it!

DENYING GOD'S PROMISES

I recall an article in one of our leading evangelical magazines a couple of years ago, debating whether God still grants the gifts of the Spirit today. (The gifts of the Spirit, of course, are listed several times in Paul's letters; they include such things as preaching, teaching, prophecy, and healing. See the list in 1 Corinthians 12:4–11, for example.) On the "pro" side of the debate was an Episcopal priest. He believed that God still gives Holy Spirit gifts to His people today, including the gift of healing. On the "con" side of the argument was a well-known evangelist. He felt that God stopped giving these gifts to His people long ago because we don't need them anymore.

I wonder what a person like this evangelist does when he gets sick? Does he say, "I know this sickness must come from You, Lord, so I'm going to pray for more sickness"? Does he say, "Please don't make me well, Lord, because that would be a bad testimony"? I doubt it. Even the people who deny God's promise of healing will turn to Him for healing when they get ill.

Others deny that God will heal *certain kinds* of illness. For example, if they have an emotional problem they don't go to the church for prayer; they go to a mental health clinic or a psychiatrist. If a friend or relative goes insane, they would never call a pastor to pray for that person. They seem to think that God can ease pain or heal a broken family, but mental disorders are too big for Him! So they cut themselves off from God's blessings.

> *Even those who deny God's promise of healing will turn to Him for healing when they get ill.*

Or how about the people who think God can't cure a common cold? They testify about what God can do for serious illnesses, then turn around and say, "Guess I'd better not send my children to school this week. They'll catch the flu from everybody else." Or they may say, "I'll probably come down with a cold, like everybody at work. It's that time of year." They talk like that all through the week, then come to church a couple of hours on Sunday and expect to have their faith lifted!

If we are the children of God, let's start acting like it. Let's not say what the rest of the world is saying; let's not buy the skepticism of everyone else. We don't need to expect a heart attack to strike us down, or a tumor to kill us. We worship *Jehovah-Repheka,* the LORD who heals. So let's start taking Him at His Word.

IS PAIN YOUR GOD?

Ill people become depressed very easily. They grow weary of the daily suffering. They tend to feel defeated by their illness; they fail to look to the Lord, who can conquer their illness. Visit the cancer ward in your local hospital, talk with some of the patients, and you'll see what I mean. It's not easy to struggle with pain for months, even years, without seeing some improvement. After a while, the sufferer wants to give up.

In a case like that, healing can only begin when the sufferer shakes off the depression and begins expecting to be healed. Norman Cousins, former editor of *Saturday Review,* tells about an experience he had with a serious illness.[1] He was stricken with a rare disease that destroys the muscles and joints. His doctors said they couldn't cure him; only about five percent of the victims ever recovered, and no one knew why they did.

But Mr. Cousins didn't give up. He decided he was going to get better. He decided he was going to be one of the five percent who survived. He read all the medical articles he could find about his illness; in fact, he became an expert on it. He recommended that his doctor give him a treatment that had never been tried before, and it worked. He recovered.

As far as I know, Mr. Cousins doesn't claim to be a Christian. He didn't call on the Lord to be healed, though I'm sure his healing came from the Lord. *"Every good gift and every perfect gift is from...the Father"* (James 1:17). The important thing we can learn from his experience is this: *He did not surrender to his illness.* He decided he was going to get well, and he never let go of that goal.

So often I've heard Christians say from their hospital beds, "I guess it's just the Lord's will for me to die." Yet they are young, gifted, capable people who could give many more years to the Lord's work.

> *Either pain is your god, or God is your God.*

They give up so easily. They surrender to the pain. They let their illness become the master of their lives.

Either pain is your god, or God is your God. Either circumstance is your god, or God is your God. Which is it?

God made us free moral agents with the power to choose what we will do with our lives. But I'm amazed at the choices most people make! We can choose to believe in God, but most people choose not to. We can choose to be saved from our sins, but most people choose not to. We can choose to be healed of our illnesses, but most people choose not to. I'm afraid that, for most people, the freedom to choose a miracle is so scary that they choose to suffer and die without it.

When you surrender to your circumstances, or you give in to your disease, it means you're afraid to live on the front lines of the spiritual battlefield. You head for the rear to patch yourself up after you've been beaten. That's where too many Christians spend their time—getting "patched up" from what the devil has done to them all week long. People come to me and say, "Pastor, pray for me. The devil's really been after me this week."

How about it? Is the devil influencing your life, or is God in charge of it? Is the tormentor in control, or is the Healer in control? You must decide. The depression, sorrow, and confusion that Satan gives will come upon you only if you let them come upon you.

Praise God for being *Jehovah-Repheka*. Thank Him for being the One who *"healeth all thy diseases."* Then claim His healing for *your* life today!

NOTES

1. Norman Cousins, *Anatomy of an Illness* (New York: W. W. Norton and Company, 1979).

CHAPTER 8

THE LORD IS OUR RIGHTEOUSNESS (JEHOVAH-TSIDQENU)

I am amazed when I talk with brilliant scientists who work with the mysteries of life in their laboratories and yet curse the coworkers beside them. I am puzzled that genius-level astronomers and physicists can explore the depths of space and yet care nothing about the bums on Skid Row. I am dismayed to see a mechanic adjust the fine workings of his automobile and yet scream all sorts of insults at his wife. The psalmist said, *"The heavens declare the glory of God; and the firmament showeth his handiwork"* (Psalm 19:1). Yet millions of people gaze upon miracles every day and fail to see God. They don't change their lives one whit; they are irascible sinners, day in and day out.

Jesus said that this natural world reveals the heavenly Father who made it, whether sinful humanity realizes that or not. Moreover, the Bible says God will hold us accountable for the corrupt way that we live in the face of this abundant evidence of God's existence. (See Romans 1.) God is a holy, righteous God; and He expects us to be righteous as well.

GOD'S EVIDENCE AND MAN'S VERDICT

Josh McDowell has written a tremendous book entitled *Evidence That Demands a Verdict,* in which he lists dozens of proofs that God exists.[1] I hope you read that book someday; it will inspire and challenge you. But even if you never read McDowell's book, you read God's own book of "proofs" every day because you live in the world He created. Jesus said,

> *Behold the fowls of the air: for they sow not, neither do they reap, nor gather into barns; yet your heavenly Father feedeth them. Are ye not much better than they?...And why take ye thought for raiment? Consider the lilies of the field, how they grow; they toil not, neither do they spin: and yet I say unto you, That even Solomon in all his glory was not arrayed like one of these. Wherefore, if God so clothe the grass of the field, which to day is, and to morrow is cast into the oven, shall he not much more clothe you, O ye of little faith?* (Matthew 6:26, 28–30)

The order of the natural world shows that Someone is in charge of things; Someone cares about every detail of the universe, even to the feeding of the sparrows. Logic would say that these birds should have died long ago of hunger and exposure, but they haven't. The theory of evolution would say that plants as tender and delicate as the lilies would have been crowded out by tough, aggressive weeds; but they haven't. Someone cares for the sparrows and lilies. That Someone is God, and He cares for you even more.

> Someone cares for the sparrows and lilies. That Someone is God, and He cares for you even more.

Yet many people study the wonders of this intricate world every day and never perceive God. A prize-winning scientist recently boasted:

> A Designer is a natural, appealing, and altogether human explanation of the biological world. But, as Darwin and Wallace showed, there is another way, equally appealing, equally human, and far more appealing: natural selection [i.e., evolution], which makes the music of life more beautiful as the aeons pass.[2]

Obviously, this man's careful study of nature did not automatically make him believe in God. This attitude is fairly common among scientists today.

That is why God revealed Himself to His people in dramatic, unmistakable ways—like through the burning bush. That is also why God revealed His written Word to us, to explain what the natural world means in case we fail to perceive who is behind it all!

One thing should be clear: God likes order and harmony. He made such a beautifully well-ordered world because He likes to arrange things that way. The same is true of human society; He wants order and harmony among people because that will protect the creatures He made and allow them to serve Him as they should. God gave His people laws to make sure they live in an orderly way. He punishes their unlawful, immoral conduct because He knows it will destroy all of us if He allows it to go unchecked. Divine law and moral decency are safeguards for the survival of humankind; they help to insure that men and women can live as God intended, without undue harm befalling them.

Man's Mechanism for Self-Destruction

But humankind is not inclined to follow God's law. Isn't that strange? Canadian geese follow their instincts and fly south for the winter, salmon follow their instincts and swim upstream to spawn, but the human race won't follow God's natural order for their life. People disregard God's law. They insist on living their own way, regardless of what God says is best. The result? People tend to destroy themselves, like a missile with a mechanism for self-destruction that blows itself up when it strays off course.

The human race is destroying itself by straying from God's revealed law.

One sign of that self-destruction is the rise of militarism in our world. I believe military leaders will be held accountable for the frightful atrocities they are inflicting, either directly or indirectly, upon innocent families. When I think of the billions of dollars spent on weapons each year—dollars that could have been spent on food and clothing for millions of needy people around the world—my heart is dismayed. I'm sure God is angry. The destroyers of earth spend so much to devise new instruments of war, when the real need of individuals is to understand and love other people! What a pathetic sign of human carnality! But Christ will return to this world soon, to destroy the destroyers. Jesus said, *"All who take the sword will perish by the sword"* (Matthew 26:52 NKJV). This is the destiny of everyone who defies God's gospel of peace.

Death is also the destiny of the less aggressive enemies of God. Whom do I mean by that? I mean everyone who disobeys God in less obvious ways, or who simply neglects to obey the mandates of His Word; in other words, everyone who sins against God. Scripture says, *"For the wages of sin is death, but the gift of God is eternal life in Christ Jesus our Lord"* (Romans 6:23 NKJV). Sin is any willful transgression of God's law, so a person may sin by defying what God says or just by ignoring what He says. But God's Word is clear and direct; God's commands are easy to understand. We can be sure that any man or woman who disobeys His Word will reap the consequences.

I have visited city missions in some of the great metropolitan areas of our nation; and in every one of them, I have found pathetic portraits of this human self-destruction through sin. Whether in Chicago, New York, Los Angeles, or right here in South Bend, the story of sin-wrecked lives is repeated again and again.

> We can be sure that any man or woman who disobeys His Word will reap the consequences.

A boy drops out of school to feed his drug habit. He "graduates" from marijuana to cocaine, and from cocaine to heroin or one of the other hard drugs. He must rob stores and mug innocent pedestrians to get enough money to buy his "fix" every day. His arms and legs are scarred with the tracks of the needle. His eyes are bloodshot with fatigue. His breath is vile. He may be fortunate to find his way into a rescue mission where Christian people can help him get right with the Lord and kick his drug habit. Otherwise he is destined to die in the gutter before he is thirty.

A girl begins running with the crowd that likes to drink. She goes to every party she can find, cracking off-color jokes and wheedling as many beers as she can get.

She frequents the neighborhood bars, soliciting drinks from the other customers and even selling sexual favors for a drink. Her habit deepens. Her nerves become raw. Like the drug addict, she is doomed to die unless someone leads her to the Lord and helps her to "dry out."

A man or woman who tries to live without God is committing suicide. It may be a slow and painful death, but the end result is certain: *"The wages of sin is death."* People destroy themselves when they ignore the clear testimony of God seen in the world He has created and in the written Word He has inspired. They are *"without excuse"* for rebelling against Him (Romans 1:20), and they must pay the penalty.

Corrupt Leadership

Laypeople are not the only ones who ignore God's commands. Even spiritual leaders, the so-called "anointed of the Lord," can be guilty of disobeying God's law. And when spiritual leaders fall into sin, they pay the same price—death.

At one of the telethons for our TV station in Miami, a precious Christian couple came to me. "Brother Sumrall, will you pray for us?" they pleaded. "We belong to one of the largest churches in southern Florida, and our pastor has been caught in adultery. Three women in the congregation have given signed statements that the pastor has committed adultery with them. He wants us to have a business meeting with him tonight to discuss these things. But we don't know what to do." Tears were running down their cheeks. I would guess they were in their fifties, handsomely dressed, and they were on their way to this important meeting with their pastor. The situation was grievous.

God expects the leaders of His church to live clean, righteous lives before His people. Christians must have holy leaders. And when we don't have them, the Bible says,

> Woe be unto the pastors that destroy and scatter the sheep of my pasture! saith the LORD....Ye have scattered my flock, and driven them away, and have not visited them: behold, I will visit upon you the evil of your doings, saith the LORD.   (Jeremiah 23:1–2)

God will not leave His church in the hands of corrupt leaders. He will not let ungodly men and women pervert the morals of His people. Not by any means! Notice what God says in that same passage:

> Behold, the days come, saith the LORD, that I will raise unto David a righteous Branch, and a King shall reign and prosper, and shall execute judgment and justice in the earth.   (Jeremiah 23:5)

The "Branch," of course, is Jesus Christ. He has fulfilled this prophecy in one sense by being born from the lineage of David. But the real thrust of this prophecy will be fulfilled when Christ returns to rule the world. He will snatch the church from the hands of every ungodly leader who pretends to be leading her in His name. He will expose these frauds for what they really are, and give them their just reward.

> *In his days Judah shall be saved, and Israel shall dwell safely: and this is his name whereby he shall be called, THE LORD OUR RIGHTEOUSNESS.*
>
> (Jeremiah 23:6)

What a majestic thought! "The LORD our righteousness"! All heaven and earth will rejoice in His righteousness. All people will realize that any righteousness Christians have is merely the "imputed" righteousness of Christ. (See Romans 4:13–25.) They will know that He is *Jehovah-Tsidqenu,* "the LORD our righteousness." This is the name God's people will use to hail Christ when He returns.

> All heaven and earth will rejoice in His righteousness.

The rest of Jeremiah 23 presents a sad commentary on human society, for it predicts that both prophet and priest will become morally profane.

✗ people know that now esp saved people

For both prophet and priest are profane; yea, in my house have I found their wickedness, saith the LORD. Wherefore their way shall be unto them as slippery ways in the darkness: they shall be driven on, and fall therein: for I will bring evil upon them.

(Jeremiah 23:11–12)

I believe there is a tremendous amount of sin in the pulpits of America today. *because the pastors are not saved!*

God, however, wants to become our righteousness; He wants to give us the holiness that we can never achieve on our own. He has already done it. He has already saved our soul from the pit of hell by sending His Son, Jesus, to die in our place. Jesus' death on the cross cleanses us of our moral impurity when we surrender our lives to Him and say, "I confess I can't live as I should. Take over my life, Lord. Make me what You want me to be." *He becomes our righteousness at the moment of conversion*

Then when we enter the gates of heaven, we won't say, "We're here because we've been so good." No, we'll walk through those gates singing a new song: "The LORD is our righteousness." He has made everything right with God the Father, with our fellowman, and even with our innermost selves. He has straightened out our lives.

DON'T WAIT TO GET RIGHT

Now some people may think, "I'll just wait until the millennium to live a holy life. That's when the Lord will *that will be too late* 142 *because the rapture would have alread accurred + they would have be left behind — lost!*

reign, isn't it? So that's when I'll let Him make me perfect."

Well, I have some exciting news for you! You don't have to wait! God is ready to make you perfect, *right now!*

↳ We are not saved to perfection

God the Father demands an upright, holy life of all His people. He expects them to be *"a peculiar people, zealous of good works"* (Titus 2:14).

God the Son died on the cross so we could become those *"peculiar,"* holy people. He purified us by sacrificing His own body and blood on Calvary. (See 1 John 1:7.) We need only confess our sin and accept His sacrifice to receive the righteousness He offers.

> *The Spirit of God keeps guiding us on the path of moral rightness.*

God the Spirit keeps guiding us on the path of moral rightness. When Paul rebuked the immorality of the Christians at Corinth, he said, *"Do you not know that you are the temple of God and that the Spirit of God dwells in you?"* (1 Corinthians 3:16 NKJV). When the Spirit dwells within, He shows us how to keep our *"temple"* clean.

It's not necessary for you to wait until the Lord Jesus returns before you get your moral life straightened out. In fact, it's downright dangerous to wait. You can live in God's righteousness now, and *"to him who knows to do good and does not do it, to him it is sin"* (James 4:17 NKJV).

Hal Lindsey closes his classic book on prophecy, *The Late Great Planet Earth,* with a reminder that none of us should wait to live as God has told us to:

> We should make it our aim to trust Christ to work in us a life of true righteousness. We all grow in this, so don't get discouraged or forget that God accepts us as we are. He wants our hearts to be constantly set toward pleasing Him and have faith to trust Him to help us.[3]

Granted, none of us will be completely perfect until our raptured bodies go to heaven. But we can have the righteousness of God, through Christ, at this very moment. God expects us to have it because He expects His church—the family of all the saved—to be *"a glorious church, not having spot, or wrinkle, or any such thing; but that it should be holy and without blemish"* (Ephesians 5:27).

We can have that kind of life only when we surrender to Jesus Christ, "the LORD our righteousness."

NOTES

1. Josh McDowell, *Evidence That Demands a Verdict* (San Bernardino, Calif.: Campus Crusade for Christ, 1971).

2. Carl Sagan, *Cosmos* (New York: Random House, 1980), p. 29.

3. Hal Lindsey and C. C. Carlson, *The Late Great Planet Earth* (Grand Rapids, Mich.: Zondervan Publishing House, 1970), p. 187.

CHAPTER 9

THE LORD OF HOSTS
(JEHOVAH-TSEBAOTH)

B efore mankind was on the face of this earth, cosmic battles took place. The beginning of all war was not on this earth, it was in heaven. Michael, God's warring archangel, and the armies of God fought against Lucifer and his angels. Revelation 12 outlines the battle and how Lucifer with one-third of the angels were cast out of heaven to the earth. These fallen angels are the demons that torment humans until this day.

And there was war in heaven: Michael and his angels fought against the dragon; and the dragon fought and his angels, and prevailed not; neither was their place found any more in heaven. And the great dragon was cast out, that old serpent, called the Devil, and Satan, which deceiveth the whole world: he was cast out into the earth, and his angels were cast out with him.

(Revelation 12:7–9)

War in Heaven

This was the beginning of all war in heaven when an angel, a created being, decided to be like the Creator.

> *How art thou fallen from heaven, O Lucifer, son of the morning! how art thou cut down to the ground, which didst weaken the nations! For thou hast said in thine heart, I will ascend into heaven, I will exalt my throne above the stars of God: I will sit also upon the mount of the congregation, in the sides of the north: I will ascend above the heights of the clouds; I will be like the most High.* (Isaiah 14:12–14)

[handwritten: NOT]
[handwritten: but not equal]

Ezekiel gives us a further illumination of Lucifer's fall.

[handwritten in margin: all these jewels reflect light the Shekinah but have no light of their own]
[handwritten in margin: music]

> *Son of man, take up a lamentation upon the king of Tyrus, and say unto him, Thus saith the Lord God; Thou sealest up the sum, full of wisdom, and perfect in beauty. Thou hast been in Eden the garden of God; every precious stone was thy covering, the sardius, topaz, and the diamond, the beryl, the onyx, and the jasper, the sapphire, the emerald, and the carbuncle, and gold: the workmanship of thy tabrets and of thy pipes was prepared in thee in the day that thou wast created. Thou art the anointed cherub that covereth; and I have set thee so: thou wast upon the holy mountain of God; thou hast walked up and down in the midst of the stones of fire. Thou wast perfect in thy*

148

[handwritten: my notes 7/1/2011]

ways from the day that thou wast <u>created</u>, till iniquity
was found in thee.   (Ezekiel 28:12–15)

God reminded Lucifer of the position and the blessings
he forfeited because he <u>sinned</u> against the Most High. War
arose in heaven that had to be fought and terminated.

Let us examine God's function in the area of war.

ARCHANGELS OF THE LORD OF HOSTS

In the structure of heaven, God created archangels:
Gabriel, Michael, and Lucifer.

Gabriel is in charge of
heaven's telecommunica-
tions. Scripture records
three instances where Ga-
briel appeared to humans.
It was Gabriel who brought
the word to Mary concern-
ing the birth of Jesus (Luke
1:26). Gabriel appeared to
Zachariah in Luke 1:18 re-
garding John the Baptist's
birth and ministry. Gabriel also spoke to Daniel about end-
time prophecy in Daniel chapters 8 and 9.

> *God reminded Lucifer of the position and blessings he forfeited because he sinned.*

Michael is the <u>warrior angel</u>. When Daniel prayed, he
entered into spiritual warfare:

*But the prince of the kingdom of Persia withstood me
one and twenty days: but, lo, Michael, one of the chief
princes, came to help me; and I remained there with
the kings of Persia.* (Daniel 10:13)

Satan became personified in kingships such as in Babylon, Persia, and Greece; and he designated these kingdoms as his domain (Daniel 10:20). *don't forget Rome*

Lucifer was the archangel in charge of song and praise in heaven; however, he rebelled. The angel who led worship decided he was as great as God and would elevate himself. *He didn't want to lead worship of, but wanted to be worshipped. NOT!!*

*O LORD of hosts, God of Israel, that dwellest between
the cherubims, thou art the God, even thou alone, of
all the kingdoms of the earth: thou hast made heaven
and earth.* (Isaiah 37:16)

THE LORD OF HOSTS IS A WARRIOR *yeah!*

The term LORD of Hosts is cited 282 times in the Word of God. It is a military term meaning "God of Battles."

*As birds flying, so will the LORD of hosts defend Jerusalem; defending also he will deliver it; and passing
over he will preserve it.* (Isaiah 31:5)

Our God is a Warrior. He is a Fighter, and we are in His army. When He comes, riding upon a white horse, His army will be with him to battle the Antichrist (Revelation

19:14). As children of the LORD of Hosts, we are following after the One who wins every battle.

A struggle is not bad if it's for a good purpose. God wants warriors who stand up for Him in the face of the enemy so that the lost may be saved. That is the most important battle we face.

One reason we see weakness in the body of Christ is because we often fail to acknowledge the LORD of Hosts, the God of Battles. Many Christians think that once they are saved, their battle with sin and Satan is over. But actually, the call to salvation is a call to enlist in God's army and war against the spirits of darkness and their activity in this world. It's a never-ending fight.

> Many Christians think that once they are saved, their battle with sin and Satan is over.

We must understand His character to appreciate the LORD of Hosts. The LORD of Battles can tell us exactly how to stand against the strategies of the enemy. He can counsel us on how to fight and how to win our victories.

This also cometh forth from the LORD of hosts, which is wonderful in counsel, and excellent in working.

(Isaiah 28:29)

LORD OF SABAOTH, "THE LORD OF ARMIES"

The LORD of Hosts is referred to in the New Testament as the LORD of Armies:

Behold, the hire of the labourers who have reaped down your fields, which is of you kept back by fraud, crieth: and the cries of them which have reaped are entered into the ears of the Lord of sabaoth.

(James 5:4)

And as Esaias said before, Except the Lord of Sabaoth had left us a seed, we had been as Sodoma, and been made like unto Gomorrha. (Romans 9:29)

If it were not for God's holiness in defeating the devil for us through Jesus Christ at Calvary, we would be eternally lost in sin. He is the LORD of Armies who wins the battles for us.

THE LORD OF HOSTS KEEPS HIS PROMISES

Every year Elkanah and his barren wife, Hannah, traveled to Shiloh to bring their sacrifice and offerings before the LORD of Hosts. In great need and intense prayer, Hannah made a commitment to the LORD of Hosts:

And she vowed a vow, and said, O LORD of hosts, if thou wilt indeed look on the affliction of thine handmaid, and remember me, and not forget thine handmaid, but

wilt give unto thine handmaid a man child, then I
will give him unto the LORD all the days of his life,
and there shall no razor come upon his head.

(1 Samuel 1:11)

The LORD of Hosts heard Hannah's cry, and the great prophet Samuel was conceived. Samuel was pivotal in the plan of God. He consummated a dispensation of 450 years and fifteen judges and ended the era when he anointed David, the warrior, as King of Israel (Acts 13:20).

For the LORD of hosts hath purposed, and who shall
disannul it? and his hand is stretched out, and who
shall turn it back?   (Isaiah 14:27)

DAVID KNEW THE LORD OF HOSTS

David not only knew Jehovah-Rohi as his Shepherd, he also recognized Jehovah-Tsebaoth—the LORD of Hosts. David trusted in God's ability to fight his enemies and win his battles for him. He became the champion of his nation and a legend in his own time through the LORD of Hosts.

Then said David to the Philistine, Thou comest to
me with a sword, and with a spear, and with a
shield: but I come to thee in the name of the LORD
of hosts, the God of the armies of Israel, whom thou
hast defied. This day will the LORD deliver thee into

153

mine hand; and I will smite thee, and take thine head from thee; and I will give the carcases of the host of the Philistines this day unto the fowls of the air, and to the wild beasts of the earth; that all the earth may know that there is a God in Israel. And all this assembly shall know that the LORD saveth not with sword and spear: for the battle is the Lord's, and he will give you into our hands.

(1 Samuel 17:45–47)

> David's bold response to Goliath was a response of faith in the Lord of Hosts.

David's bold response to Goliath was a response of faith in the LORD of Hosts. In the book of Psalms, David referred to the LORD of Hosts fifteen times. He knew the LORD of Hosts could bring him the blessings he needed. *"O LORD of hosts, blessed is the man that trusteth in thee"* (Psalm 84:12).

THE LORD OF HOSTS JUDGES NATIONS

But, O LORD of hosts, that judgest righteously, that triest the reins and the heart, let me see thy vengeance on them: for unto thee have I revealed my cause.

(Jeremiah 11:20)

For the day of the LORD of hosts shall be upon every one that is proud and lofty, and upon every one that is lifted up; and he shall be brought low.

(Isaiah 2:12)

And I will come near to you to judgment; and I will be a swift witness against the sorcerers, and against the adulterers, and against false swearers, and against those that oppress the hireling in his wages, the widow, and the fatherless, and that turn aside the stranger from his right, and fear not me, saith the LORD of hosts. (Malachi 3:5)

God is speaking against transgressors, rebellious people who will not serve Him.

The Soviet Union fought God for over seventy years with their lips and actions. It was torn asunder from within, and reaped what it sowed.

America has experienced God's blessings only because our forefathers loved and served Him. They attended church and hated sin. Because of this, our generation is reaping a harvest that we didn't plant. One day our children will reap the harvest we are now planting; so let's be deliberate in what we plant before the LORD of Hosts.

Their Redeemer is strong; the LORD of hosts is his name: he shall thoroughly plead their cause, that he may give rest to the land, and disquiet the inhabitants of Babylon. (Jeremiah 50:34)

THE LORD'S HOSTS HAVE A CAPTAIN

Not only does the LORD of Hosts have volunteers in His army, He has a Captain.

And it came to pass, when Joshua was by Jericho, that he lifted up his eyes and looked, and, behold, there stood a man over against him with his sword drawn in his hand: and Joshua went unto him, and said unto him, Art thou for us, or for our adversaries? And he said, Nay; but as captain of the host of the LORD am I now come. And Joshua fell on his face to the earth, and did worship, and said unto him, What saith my lord unto his servant? And the captain of the LORD's host said unto Joshua, Loose thy shoe from off thy foot; for the place whereon thou standest is holy. And Joshua did so. (Joshua 5:13–15)

> Only the Most High is worthy of praise.

We know that this person with a sword in his hand was not an angel because angels refuse worship. Only the Most High is worthy of praise; however, this Mighty One commanded Joshua to worship Him. The Captain of God's hosts is Jesus Christ.

When the children of Israel faced their first battle after coming into the Promised Land, the LORD of Hosts took over the warfare.

156

THE LORD OF HOSTS (JEHOVAH-TSEBAOTH)

Archaeologists have discovered that the walls of Jericho did not fall east or west, they fell straight down. It's no wonder. When Jesus hits any wall, it must come down!

Thus saith the LORD the King of Israel, and his redeemer the LORD of hosts; I am the first, and I am the last; and beside me there is no God. (Isaiah 44:6)

[handwritten: *The Father*]
[handwritten: *the Lord Jesus*]

Jesus teaches His people how to fight. For the church, this means spiritual warfare.

WE ARE IN SPIRITUAL WARFARE

It is very interesting that the first instrument used against man after he sinned in Genesis chapter 3 was an angel with a sword. This indicates that cosmic warfare is ongoing.

So he drove out the man; and he placed at the east of the garden of Eden Cherubims, and a flaming sword which turned every way, to keep the way of the tree of life. (Genesis 3:24)

For we wrestle not against flesh and blood, but against principalities, against powers, against the rulers of the darkness of this world, against spiritual wickedness in high places. (Ephesians 6:12)

Our warfare is spiritual. It is not against people, but against the powers of darkness. Some Christians refuse to

[handwritten: * they are in the warfare automatically whether they want to be or not!]

get into the area of spiritual warfare, and some have been carried away by extremes.

Many have become weary practicing spiritual warfare. They are fighting the devil and trying to win a battle that is already won. What they need to do is to shout and rejoice in God. Jesus triumphed over Satan and destroyed his works at Calvary. Satan's only weapon now against mankind is deception.

"And having spoiled principalities and powers, he made a show of them openly, triumphing over them in it" (Colossians 2:15).

> Jesus triumphed over Satan and destroyed his works at Calvary.

When man tries to enter into a personal conflict against Satan using human strength, he can never win. But we must exercise spiritual warfare according to the Word of God. James 4:7 admonishes us, *"Submit yourselves therefore to God. Resist the devil, and he will flee from you."*

You and I have the victory because of Jesus. We function and operate through His successes and through His victories. Our victories are not accomplished through human manipulation, but by the LORD of Hosts. He is the One who has defeated the devil! He is the Almighty God!

Anchor your trust in the LORD of Hosts. Depend upon Him. He is the LORD of Battles. He is the LORD of Victories. Call on Him by His Name, and ask Him to do what He is capable of doing. Say, "Lord, You are the Mighty Deliverer. I've got some enemies. ~~Go get 'em!"~~ *We request, we don't command; He is God not us*

I believe that in these last days, spiritual warfare ~~will~~ *is* be intensified. More and more, wickedness and viciousness will come against us. The body of Christ is going to bless the world. We are going to stand up with Jesus in all of His strength and win every battle!

> For thus saith the LORD of hosts; Yet once, it is a little while, and I will shake the heavens, and the earth, and the sea, and the dry land; and I will shake all nations, and the desire of all nations shall come: and I will fill this house with glory, saith the LORD of hosts. The silver is mine, and the gold is mine, saith the LORD of hosts. The glory of this latter house shall be greater than of the former, saith the LORD of hosts: and in this place will I give peace, saith the LORD of hosts.
> (Haggai 2:6–9)

✗ No we aren't 159 *because so many churches are compromised*

CHAPTER 10

THE LORD IS CONQUEROR
(JEHOVAH-NISSI)

I n previous chapters, we have studied the names of God
that He revealed to individuals such as Melchizedek,
Abraham, and Moses at some crisis in their lives. The
following chapters are a bit different because they will discuss place names that Old Testament people gave to certain places to declare what they learned about God there.

Turn in your Bible to Exodus 17. This chapter tells
how the children of Israel pitched their tents at Rephidim
after years of wandering through the wilderness. If you
check a Bible atlas, you will find that Rephidim is a rugged
desert Place near Mount Horeb. Water is scarce there, and
the Bible says that when the Israelites arrived at Rephidim, *"there was no water for the people to drink"* (Exodus
17:1). The people were weary of wandering, the armies of
Amalek were pressing down upon them, and there was not
so much as a drop of good drinking water for them. They

felt utterly defeated. So they started complaining to Moses once again.

If you are a pastor, you probably know exactly how Moses felt. A congregation goes through its "dry desert places," just as the Israelites did. At times, the people of God run up against one dead end after another and one problem after another. There seems to be no relief in sight. They come to their pastor with a complaining spirit and say, "Do we have to keep on going? Do we have to keep on fighting this battle for the Lord? Looks like the Lord has given up on us, so let's admit we're licked."

> Defeatism can overwhelm God's people and make them lay down their weapons.

Defeatism is a curse. It can overwhelm God's people and make them lay down their weapons, even before the battle has begun. Moses, however, was not about to be defeated. He took the problem straight to the Lord and cried, *"What shall I do unto this people? they be almost ready to stone me"* (Exodus 17:4). He didn't lean on his own human wisdom. He didn't run to some textbook on church administration, or to some leadership expert. He turned to the Lord. In effect, he said, "You brought us out here, Lord. Now You will have to take care of us. So what do You want me to do?"

162

If more of God's leaders did that today, we would see fewer people leaving the church, disgusted because of the trouble they find there. God Himself gives us the best answers when God's people run up against a problem.

God told Moses what to do. He directed Moses to a certain rock and told him to strike the rock with the staff that he had used to part the Red Sea. Moses did as God told him, and water gushed out of the rock to give the Israelites plenty to drink.

This occured not a moment too soon because the Amalekites descended upon them. (See Exodus 17:8.) Moses turned to his commander-in-chief, Joshua, and told him to muster an army against these invaders: *"Choose us out men, and go out, fight with Amalek: to morrow I will stand on the top of the hill with the rod of God in mine hand"* (verse 9). The armies of Amalek had come out to destroy the Israelites, but Moses knew God wanted them to enter the Promised Land. So nobody could stop them. Nobody could destroy them. You can be sure that no one can destroy you one moment before God is through using you. If He has called you to evangelize the continent of Africa (as He did with David Livingstone), you can be sure He won't let you die until you've gone to Africa and preached the Word. If God has called you to live in another country (as He did with the Israelites), you can be sure you won't be destroyed before you get a chance to set up housekeeping there.

Moses knew that, so he wasn't afraid. He told Joshua that he would stand atop the mountain and raise the rod of God to remind the Israelites who was fighting for them that day. God was! Aaron and Hur had to help him hold up his hands, but he kept his promise. And God kept His. The Israelites defeated the Amalekites that day. Moses then built an altar to commemorate the great victory they had won. Notice what the Bible says about that monument:

> *Jehovah-Nissi means "the Lord is my banner," or "the Lord is my sign of conquest."*

And Moses built an altar, and called the name of it Jehovahnissi ["the LORD my banner"]: for he said, Because the LORD hath sworn that the LORD will have war with Amalek from generation to generation.
> (Exodus 17:15–16)

Jehovah-Nissi—what an unusual thing to say about God! This name means "the LORD is my banner," or "the LORD is my sign of conquest." In other words, Moses used this name to declare that God would always conquer the foes of His people. As long as Moses and the Israelites followed the LORD, they would have victory. He would defeat the Amalekites and any other pagan people who tried to thwart His purpose and plan.

What's Your Banner?

People march under different "banners" today. They put their trust in different things; they give credit for their success to different things. What do you credit for making you who you are today? *To the Lord Jesus Christ everything I have belongs to Him + is because of Him*

Perhaps you credit your brains. You think you acquired the wonderful mate you live with, the fancy home you live in, the swanky car you drive, and the well-paying job you have with brains! After every new business deal, you think to yourself, "Am I not clever? Didn't I outfox them again?" You go through life under the banner of "Brains" or "Intellect." You tell other people that you got where you are today by "outsmarting" your competitors.

Or perhaps you credit your success to your physical strength or your great physique. Perhaps your friends have said, "He's as strong as an ox," and you like that reputation. You want to convince your boss and everyone else that you have more endurance than other people, so you like to work overtime. You like to tackle the toughest assignments. You like to show everyone how much physical stamina you have. And then you like to say, in mock modesty, "I can handle it." You're marching under the banner of "Brawn" or "Strength."

Perhaps your banner is money, or arrogance, or "knowing the right people." You credit these things for the successes you have in life. They are the banners you hold up as you march on to your personal victories.

But all these things will fail you someday. Advancing age will weaken your brain and rob your muscles of strength. Inflation will suck your money out of the bank. Fickle human nature will turn your friends against you. Repeated failures will give a hollow ring to your arrogance. March under any of these banners, and you will follow it to defeat.

GOD'S RIGHTFUL PLACE—IN FRONT

Moses learned that when he followed God, he conquered. When he let God blaze the trail before him, he had victory. Moses learned to let God be his leader from bondage to the Promised Land. And so should we.

Christians fail to have victory in life when they won't let God be their banner. Sometimes they want God to follow along behind them, blessing whatever they decide to do. They pray, "Lord, bless what I do today in Your name." But that kind of attitude puts God in the wrong place. It puts Him in the chuckwagon, bringing up the rear of the battle column, when He should be the Captain at the front of the column.

Ken Forsch, a pitcher for the Houston Astros baseball team, had to learn this lesson the hard way. During the 1977 playing season, he injured his right arm. Although the doctors and trainers were able to relieve the pain, he lost most of the strength he needed in that arm. For the rest of the season, he was a lousy pitcher.

He did no better at the start of the 1978 season. Every time he came to the mound, batters usually got an easy hit. Ken put himself through a grueling series of exercises to toughen his muscles, trying to regain the strength of his grip. But he didn't improve. His wife and friends prayed for him because they knew his career might soon be over.

After another dismal failure in a game against Pittsburgh, Ken went back to his hotel room and collapsed in despair. He knew all too well that the problem was too much for him to handle. He just couldn't go on in his own strength.

In quiet acceptance, he bowed his head and turned the problem over to the Lord—to do with as *He* wished. And he slept peacefully.

> In quiet acceptance, he bowed his head and turned the problem over to the Lord.

Soon the Astros met the Montreal Expos in a doubleheader. The first game tied and went into the twelfth inning with bases loaded. Then Ken was called to pitch. He promptly struck out three men and won the game. In the second game, he was called to pitch at the bottom of the eighth inning. He helped the Astros win again. After that, his coach put Ken back in the starting lineup, and he won eight of the next ten games.

On the second day of the 1979 season, Ken pitched his first no-hitter, against Atlanta. Thinking back on that experience, Ken realized what his struggle had been. He had been insistent on doing things his way, deliberately refusing to think about what God might have in mind. But Ken learned well that when he asked God to take charge, He worked his life out even better than he could have imagined.

That's what Moses and the Israelites learned at Rephidim. God the Banner must always be in front of our lives, leading the way, if we are going to have victory.

FOUR KINDS OF VICTORY

God gives us many kinds of victory. Listing all of them would be impossible in the brief space I have here, so let me point out four kinds of victory that I think every Christian should possess.

1. *God gives us victory over sin.* First John 1:7 says, *"But if we walk in the light, as he is in the light, we have fellowship one with another, and the blood of Jesus Christ his Son cleanseth us from all sin."* Notice the Bible says He cleanses us from *"all sin."* He gives us victory over every sin in our lives. He doesn't give us just a partial cleansing of sin; He washes it all away.

We had a friend on one of our Holy Land tours who stopped smoking about ten times in eleven days! I'm always puzzled to see Christians "get the victory" so many times over the same sin. I believe that when we have victory over sin, it ought to be permanent. When we knock the devil out of our lives and he starts to get up again, we should put a foot on him and say "Listen, you're down! You're out! You're finished in Jesus' name!" We don't need to repeat our victory over sin again and again because Jesus is our Banner. He has won the victory for us. We only need to claim that victory to make it ours all the time.

2. *God gives us victory over habit slavery.* This is related to our victory over sin. Jesus said, *"If the Son therefore shall make you free, ye shall be free indeed"* (John 8:36). No longer are we bound to the habits that hinder us from serving the Lord. Whether it's smoking, drinking, or even compulsive coffee-sipping—whatever the habit may be, Christ can set us free. We no longer need to be enslaved to our habits.

3. *God gives us victory over self.* Galatians 2:20 says, *"I am crucified with Christ: nevertheless I live; yet not I, but Christ liveth in me."* Here the Bible refers to our victory over the dictates of self-desire.

Lucifer was an angel of God who rebelled against God because he couldn't do things his own way. He was cast out of heaven because God would not let him follow his own willful impulses (see Isaiah 14:12–20). Ever since that time, he has tried to deceive man into following the same kind of error. He has tried to convince us that our

Sin!

own self-conceited wisdom is better than God's wisdom. Satan's deception is a lie straight from the pit of hell, but God gives us the victory over it. Jesus said, *"If any man will come after me, let him deny himself, and take up his cross, and follow me"* (Matthew 16:24). He gives us the power to conquer self-desire and self-will and to submit ourselves to the will of almighty God.

4. *God gives us victory over sorrow.* Job provides the classic example of man's struggle with sorrow. Job had so many problems that he couldn't understand, and these were perplexing because he suffered these problems while being faithful to God.

> *If we put our trust in the Lord God our banner, He will give us victory over our sorrow.*

Every one of us has problems we don't understand. Life is not always easy. But if we put our trust in the Lord God our banner, He will give us victory over the sorrow that would otherwise overwhelm us. He keeps us from groveling in grief over our problems.

I once received a ten-page letter from a friend I had met when I was a young preacher in Oklahoma. The letter described how I had baptized several people in the Arkansas River while holding a series of meetings at a country schoolhouse. My correspondent recounted how her father had made her walk eight miles every night to the schoolhouse to hear my preaching. But she had not accepted the Lord. She later married and moved to California. The night she wrote the letter, she had tried to jump off the Oakland Bridge to commit suicide. But the police had caught her.

"I want to kill myself," she told me, "because my life has been nothing but sorrow."

Here was a woman who literally had been baptized in sorrow. She heard the gospel and had an opportunity to give her heart to the Lord. But she never did so, and she has been defeated by sorrow ever since.

My book on grief tells how I struggled with a heavy grief in my own life—the deaths of five close friends in a plane crash.[2] God gave me victory over that grief. He kept me from drowning in sorrow. And I know from that personal experience that He is *Jehovah-Nissi,* "the LORD my banner," even in the face of sorrow.

Let God give you the victory today. No matter what threatens to defeat you in life, you can know that God is the Conqueror who marches on before you. If you're willing to follow Him and give Him the credit for your victory, He will let you triumph every time.

NOTES

1. Ken Forsch, "Have It Your Way, Lord." *Guideposts*. (April 1981), pp. 30–31.

2. Lester Sumrall, *You Can Conquer Grief Before It Conquers You* (Nashville: Thomas Nelson Publishers, 1981).

CHAPTER 11

THE LORD IS PEACE
(JEHOVAH-SHALOM)

During World War II, I spent three months preaching in what was then the eastern regions of Poland. I traveled through Minsk to Vilna, all the way to the Russian border. What a hair-raising experience that was! At times we could hear the hooves of the cavalry troops nearby, and my interpreter would hush my preaching. The house in which I was preaching would be completely silent. We knew that if the soldiers found that many people assembled in one place, we would all be thrown in jail.

Can you imagine how you would feel to be thrown in jail for praising the Lord?

I have preached to Christians in the jails of China. These people often had nothing but bamboo stakes for walls and a dirt floor to sleep on. They were lucky to get anything to eat. Many of them starved or were tortured to death for their faith.

Can you imagine how you would feel worshipping the Lord under those conditions?

Yet it seems that God revealed precious things about Himself to the Israelites when they worshipped Him in times of trouble. He disclosed a new name for Himself—a name that helped them understand Him better—in a time of national crisis. We find another example of this in Judges 6. This chapter opens by telling how the Midianites were destroying the fields and villages of the Israelites, making life utterly miserable for them. The Midianites wanted to drive them out of Canaan once and for all.

> *God revealed Himself when the Israelites worshipped Him in times of trouble.*

And [the Midianites] *encamped against them, and destroyed the increase of the earth, till thou come unto Gaza, and left no sustenance for Israel, neither sheep, nor ox, nor ass. For they came up with their cattle and their tents, and they came as grasshoppers for multitude; for both they and their camels were without number: and they entered into the land to destroy it.* (Judges 6:4–5)

So God sent a ~~prophet~~ to the Israelites. The Bible doesn't even record his name (see verse 8), just his message. He said:

Thus saith the LORD God of Israel, I brought you up from Egypt, and brought you forth out of the house of bondage; and I delivered you out of the hand of the Egyptians, and out of the hand of all that oppressed you, and drave them out from before you, and gave you their land; and I said unto you, I am the LORD your God; fear not the gods of the Amorites, in whose land ye dwell: but ye have not obeyed my voice.

(Judges 6:8–10)

The Israelites were worried about their enemies. But God said, "Wait a minute. Don't you remember how I brought you out of Egypt? Don't you remember the victories I gave you over the Canaanites when you first entered this land? Didn't I tell you not to be afraid of the pagan gods of these people? You're in this mess because you forgot My promises. You're afraid because you've forgotten how powerful I am."

The Power of Praise

God was reminding the Israelites of one of the most neglected spiritual truths: the power of praise. Many times we become so anxious to enlist God's help for a certain problem that we forget to thank Him for what He has already done about it. And when the problem is solved, we tend to say, "Oh well, I would have gotten those blessings anyway."

When I tell people how God healed me of tuberculosis when I was a boy, they often say, "You probably would have been healed anyway." But the doctor didn't think so. When he came to our home and examined me, he wrote out my death certificate and left it on my father's desk. "The boy can't live two more hours," he said. "You had better start digging his grave."

But God performed a miracle for me. God healed me. And I will always give Him the praise for that.

When I face an especially tough problem and begin praying about it, I start by praising God for what He's already done. My friend Merlin Carothers does the same thing. He's written several books on the power of praise.[1] As a chaplain in the Army, he found the best advice he could give men about their prayer life was this: *Start by praising God for what He's already done!* You will be surprised at the tremendous spiritual power unleashed in a thankful heart.

This prophet of God mentioned in Judges recalled the marvelous things God had done for the Israelites. In that time of national crisis, God had him preach a sermon on thankfulness. God would begin to give victory when the hearts of His people were thankful.

"The Lord Is Peace"

Then God sent an angel to draft a farm boy named Gideon into military duty. God called Gideon to be the captain of a new army that would go out to fight the Midianites. Gideon saw himself as a most unlikely candidate for that job, so God had to give him some miraculous signs to prove He was serious about the call. (See Judges 6:15–22.) At last Gideon was convinced. He accepted God's call. And he erected an altar on the spot as a monument to what God had told him:

> Then Gideon built an altar there unto the LORD, and called it Jehovahshalom [the LORD is Peace]: unto this day it is yet in Ophrah of the Abiezrites.
>
> (Judges 6:24)

What a striking name for that place! "The LORD is peace." Despite the terrible threat of the Midianite army and the meager strength of the Israelite militia that Gideon could rally against them—despite that dreadful prospect of war, Gideon knew that "the LORD is peace."

If you want to live a double life, God will let you do that.

If you want to live a double life, looking oh-so-religious in church on Sunday but living like the devil the rest of the week, God will let you do that. However, you will have no peace living that way. And you will face eternal damnation in the end for living that way. But God gives you that choice.

On the other hand, if you want to plunge into the Christian life, and if you want to love the Lord with all your heart, He will be everything to you that He was to Gideon and to the other heroes of the Bible. Scripture tells us that He is *"the same yesterday, and to day, and for ever"* (Hebrew 13:8). He will be the same God to you that He was to Gideon if you are willing to serve Him faithfully.

The rest of Judges 6 and 7 tells how God brought military peace to Israel through Gideon. You probably remember the story from your childhood Sunday school lessons. Gideon began by gathering an army of thirty-two thousand men. But God told him to keep weeding out the cowardly and clumsy until he had a force of only three hundred men. With those three hundred, some clay lamps and some trumpets, Gideon routed the Midianites from their camp and sent them scurrying back home without fighting at all! *"Thus was Midian subdued before the children of Israel, so that they lifted up their heads no more. And the country was in quietness forty years in the days of Gideon"* (Judges 8:28).

God can bring peace to a nation. America needs His peace today, just as much as Israel needed it. Our greatest conflict is not with Iraq or Iran or any other country;

our greatest conflict is with the greedy hearts of our own people. Americans are at war with themselves. They are trying to get all they can for themselves, even if they have to destroy each other to do it. Because of greed, even when America has a bumper crop of wheat, the price of bread is not reduced by one penny. In the District of Columbia, Los Angeles County, and other parts of the country, the divorce rate is now higher than the marriage rate because of human lust and pride. This nation is in turmoil because our people are ruled by their sinful nature. Only the Lord God can change our nature. Only He can bring peace to our country.

> *This nation is in turmoil because our people are ruled by their sinful nature.*

You may say, "I don't believe that. I just don't see any evidence of what you're talking about." That's just because your soul is sick with sin and needs to be healed. You need to let the Holy Spirit of God *"purge your conscience from dead works to serve the living God"* (Hebrews 9:14). Greed, lust, and pride are *"dead works."* They will give you constant agony in this life and eternal torment hereafter. You need to let the Lord purge those things out of your life so you can serve Him and have peace forevermore.

Emotional Peace

God can give a nation military peace. He also can give you a spirit of peace that comes when you know you are saved. But there's another kind of peace He can give, and perhaps it is the kind of peace you need. I'm talking about emotional peace.

Many people live controlled by their emotions. They are like waves in the ocean, sloshing up and down all the time. In the morning they may be "up," and in the afternoon they may be "down." A man comes home from work and isn't sure what condition the house will be in because he doesn't know whether his wife's emotions have been "up" or "down" today. That's pathetic. But many people live that way today. If they get up from bed feeling depressed, they wallow in depression all day. If they get charged with excitement by a bonus in their paycheck, they feel happy for awhile. Soon, however, their emotions change; and their outlook on life sloshes back the other way.

God does not intend for us to live defeated emotional lives. Notice what Paul said to his friends in Corinth, people who were apt to let their emotions run their lives:

But thanks be to God, which giveth us the victory through our Lord Jesus Christ. Therefore, my beloved brethren, be ye stedfast, unmoveable, always abounding

*in the work of the Lord, forasmuch as ye know that
your labour is not in vain in the Lord.*

(1 Corinthians 15:57–58)

We should be *"stedfast"* and *"unmoveable"* in our emotions; we should be *"always abounding in the work of the Lord."* God expects His people to live victoriously and confidently. We can't live that way on our own, but we can live that way through the grace of God, *"which giveth us the victory through our Lord Jesus Christ."*

God expects His people to live victoriously and confidently.

"Brother Sumrall," you say, "does that mean we are not going to have any problems?" NO !

No, the Bible doesn't mean that at all. But it does mean that when problems come, God will give us confidence to face those problems. He will be *Jehovah-Shalom* in our lives. He will be our peace.

NOTES

1. Merlin R. Carothers, *Prison to Praise: A Radical Prayer Concept for Changing Lives* (Plainfield, N.J.: Logos International, 1970); *Power in Praise* (Plainfield, N.J.: Logos International, 1972).

CHAPTER 12

THE LORD IS THERE
(JEHOVAH-SHAMAH)

The last verse of Ezekiel's prophecy gives us an intriguing name for God. Notice what the prophet says concerning the nature of the New Jerusalem that God revealed to him in a vision:

> *It was round about eighteen thousand measures: and*
> *the name of the city from that day shall be, The LORD*
> *is there* [Jehovah-Shamah].   (Ezekiel 48:35)

God revealed that this would be the name of the Holy City when He restores her to her former glory: *Jehovah-Shamah,* "The LORD is there." But this is not only a name for the New Jerusalem; this is a name that reveals much about the nature of God Himself.

THE LORD HAS BEEN THERE

First, the name reveals that God chooses to dwell in the Holy City. The Bible shows how God picked the ancient city of Jerusalem to be the scene of many crucial events. Here Abraham met the priest-king Melchizedek who blessed him and interceded to God for him. (See Genesis 14:18–19.) Here David brought the ark of the covenant when he recaptured the land of Canaan from the Philistines. (See 2 Samuel 6:12–19.) Here David and Solomon placed the seat of their government. (See 2 Samuel 5:5–9.) Here the returning Jews erected a new temple and reestablished the sacrificial worship of God. (See Ezra 1:1–4.) Here Jesus performed many miracles, taught in the temple, and was crucified.

> *The Lord has been there, physically and spiritually, and He will reign in the New Jerusalem forever.*

The Bible calls Jerusalem *"the throne of the LORD"* (Jeremiah 3:17), predicting that God will create a New Jerusalem to be the seat of Christ's power at the end of time. (See Revelation 21.) It is only natural, then, for the New Jerusalem to be called *Jehovah-Shamah*. The Lord has been there, physically and spiritually, and He will reign in the New Jerusalem forever.

If you have ever visited present-day Jerusalem, you know how exciting it is to walk the streets that Jesus and His disciples walked. No wonder this city attracts more pilgrims than any other religious site in the world! The air seems to tingle with the drama of biblical events. Only the most hardened heart can visit that city without sensing the atmosphere of divine purpose.

I have led several tours of the Holy Land, and I must confess that Jerusalem is my favorite stop on that tour. Every time we cross that last hill and the city comes into view, the morning sun glimmering on its bleached stone ramparts, my spine tingles with excitement. I feel like saying, *"Jehovah-Shamah,* the LORD is there," for He is there in a unique way.

THE LORD WILL BE THERE—WITH US!

Second, the name *Jehovah-Shamah* reminds us that God chooses to live among men. The New Jerusalem that Ezekiel saw was to be no ghost town; it will be teeming with God's people. The saints of all the ages will live there and worship the Lamb, *"and they shall reign for ever and ever"* (Revelation 22:5).

This is not the place to begin a detailed study of Bible prophecy. But let me at least say this: I believe the Lord Jesus Christ is coming back to this earth. I believe He will conquer Satan and all of his devilish servants once and for all. I believe He will set up His kingdom, and all of the saved peoples of earth will reign with Him. And I believe all suffering, sorrow, and pain will be abolished in that kingdom. People will no longer struggle to make a living, but will live to praise the Son of God.

Do you know why I believe these things? Because the Bible teaches them. Read the books of Ezekiel and Daniel, or the great book of Revelation, and you will see the ultimate plan of God described in vivid detail. The Lord will be there in His Kingdom, and we will be with Him! What a glorious thought!

THE LORD IS HERE—NOW!

Third, and most important for our lives today, the name *Jehovah-Shamah* reminds us that the Lord is already living among His people. He is already reigning in your heart if you are a Christian. He has already set up His throne in your life if you have surrendered your life to Him. Other people wear T-shirts promoting their favorite beer or tennis shoes, but a Christian's life should advertise who lives within. A Christian's life should say just as boldly as a T-shirt does, *"Jehovah-Shamah, the LORD is there."*

The Lord enters your life at the moment you are saved. If you are a Christian, think back to how you felt when you were converted. Didn't you feel marvelous? I was saved on the night God healed me of tuberculosis as a teenager, and I shall never forget the incredible joy that flooded my heart. Christ entered my heart that night.

But later I slipped into a bad attitude that the Lord had to correct. He called me to the ministry, but I started grumbling about "having to preach." At times I even

THE LORD IS THERE (JEHOVAH-SHAMAH)

growled at the people who came to hear me, because I would rather have preached to an empty house than to preach to real live people who could hear my mistakes. I was born again, but I had not been filled with God's Holy Spirit. When I finally received His Spirit, He cleansed that foul attitude from my life. He gave me a new love for my people, and a new zeal for the work I had been called to. "The Lord was there" in an even more powerful way when I was baptized with the Holy Spirit. *(handwritten: We are baptized w/ the Holy Spirit at salvation. period!)*

I see similarities between my experience and the progress of America. Our nation *(handwritten: regress)* has changed dramatically in the past one hundred fifty years. In the early days of America, its people were lean and strong. Most men could chop down a mighty oak with their bare hands. But today most men are so flabby that they can't even split kindling for the fireplace. We have changed spiritually, too. In the early days, a person who was saved had some dramatic changes occur in his life. He or she shed old, sinful habits and started living like the *"new creature"* God intended him or her to be (2 Corinthians 5:17).

> He gave me a new love for my people, and a new zeal for the work I had been called to.

Today, however, most people think that "getting saved" is a nice little ritual that they ought to go through, but

*(handwritten at bottom: no this is error. One receives the Holy Spirit at rebirth. See P186 at the ** Being filled is being under His control v/9 obedience)*

they don't think their lives should change much because of it. They cling to the filthy habits they had before. They make excuses for not witnessing, not tithing, and not even attending worship services. When someone got saved in the camp meetings of a hundred fifty years ago, God saved him through and through; today we have thousands of people who are satisfied to be† half-saved Christians. They confess Jesus with their lips, but you can't see any change in their lives. *Because no change has occured in the heart!*

Now I don't depreciate what God is doing in people's lives today. I know His Holy Spirit is still at work. I see Him at work in my own congregation and in many congregations I have visited. But I do think that the vast majority of professing Christians have not surrendered themselves completely to the Lord's control *that would be filled*. And I think these halfhearted Christians make a mockery of the truth when they point to their own lives and say, "The Lord is here." Because He's *not* there, ~~in any obvious way~~. *They don't say.*

I think of Charles G. Finney, who practiced law in upstate New York over a century ago. Finney had attended some camp meeting services and heard what the Lord could do with a life that was fully surrendered to Him. Finney had professed to be a Christian, and he could see some changes in his life that had occurred since he was converted. But he couldn't really say that the Lord owned him completely. Charles Finney still had control of his own life, and as long as he did, he knew that God would withhold His full blessing.

† Is he nuts! There is no such thing as half-saved; either you are or you are not!

188

One day Finney felt so convicted about his spiritual life that he locked the door of his law office, walked down the street, and climbed a wooded hill to be alone. He knelt down with the Lord and surrendered himself completely to the Holy Spirit of God. That was the beginning of a marvelous ministry for young Finney. He began preaching at great city-wide evangelistic rallies throughout the eastern United States. Finney's name has gone down in history as one of the greatest preachers this nation has ever known, because he was willing to get himself out of the driver's seat and let the Lord take command. The Lord was there.

> We must be willing to get out of the driver's seat and let the Lord take command.

The Lord can do the same with you. If you're willing to "present your body as a living sacrifice" on the altar of full commitment to the Lord, He will fill your life with Himself. He will let His Spirit shine out through your life. Your friends will no longer see the spirit of John Smith or Mary Doe in all that you do; they'll see the Spirit of Christ. The Lord will be there—in you!

The Lord Is There in Trouble

How wonderful it is to be able to say, "I have a refuge from my problems. I have Someone I can turn to. I have a Friend to comfort me, no matter what happens." That's exactly what the Lord promises to you.

The Bible says,

God is our refuge and strength, a very present help in trouble. Therefore we will not fear, even though the earth be removed, and though the mountains be carried into the midst of the sea; though its waters roar and be troubled, though the mountains shake with its swelling. (Psalm 46:1–3 NKJV)

Everything in your world may turn upside down, but the Lord will still be there to comfort and help you. That's one of the most precious promises of His word, and many times He has proven that promise to me.

As I mentioned earlier, a few years ago I lost five of my closest friends in a plane wreck.[1] The grief of that day seemed greater than I could bear. But the Lord stood by me, even then. He encouraged me when I thought I could not preach because of my sorrow. He ministered to me through the words of my wife and family and the members of my congregation. There are still times a lump forms in my throat when I think of that tragedy. But the Lord reminds me that He still loves me, and that He has those departed friends in glory with Him now.

But there is a greater friend than even our closest human ones. The Bible says, *"A man who has friends must himself be friendly, But there is a friend who sticks closer than a brother"* (Proverbs 18:24 NKJV).

That Friend is Jesus Christ. You may have many friends, and think that they'll come to your aid when you have trouble. But you might discover that most of them are "fair-weather friends." They like you and help you so long as you are prospering. But when you fall into trouble, they seem to disappear. Jesus never does. He *"sticks closer than a brother,"* even when the rest of your friends abandon you. The Lord is there in time of trouble.

THE LORD IS THERE IN LONELINESS

I must confess that I can't remember when I have ever felt lonely. Until I was seventeen years old, I was surrounded by a strong family. Then I accepted Jesus Christ as my Savior, and He's been with me ever since. He has given me friends everywhere I have traveled, because He made me part of the wonderful family of God.

When I'm in China, I think I'm Chinese. When I'm in the Philippines, I think I'm a Filipino. (I almost have to look in a mirror to realize that I'm not!) Seriously, I have found such a natural fellowship with God's people in every country of the world that I can't remember being alone as long as I have ministered in His name.

But I know that loneliness is a painful problem for many people. I have visited widows who sit at their living room windows and stare blankly for hours on end. I have met with cancer patients who seldom see their friends or relatives, and college students whose families seem to have forgotten them. We live in an age of calloused hearts, when people seem to have lost the love of family and friends that was so common just one generation ago. Millions of people are lonely because no one takes time to say, "I care about you."

But the Lord cares.

The Bible says, *"For the Lord GOD will help me; therefore shall I not be confounded...He is near that justifieth me; who will contend with me? let us stand together"* (Isaiah 50:7–8). Again it says, *"Thou art near, O LORD; and all thy commandments are truth"* (Psalm 119:151). And again, *"Seek ye the LORD while he may be found, call ye upon him while he is near"* (Isaiah 55:6). Can there be any doubt that the Lord is with you today, whether you recognize Him or not? He cares for you. He wants to help you. He is closer to you than any human being because He made you and His Spirit is speaking to you. But as long as you reject Him, you will feel lonely. You won't actually *be* alone, but you'll *feel* lonely because you shun the God who is there.

> We live in an age of calloused hearts, when people seem to have lost the love of family.

The Lord Is There (Jehovah-Shamah)

Francis A. Schaeffer has written a book titled *He Is There, and He Is Not Silent.* I think there's a marvelous truth in that title. The God we serve is *Jehovah-Shamah,* the LORD who is there, and He speaks to every one of us in our innermost spirits. Some choose to reject Him. They call themselves atheists, agnostics, or something else. But all of their high-flown intellectual arguments against the existence of God do not change the fact that He is there, within us. He is not silent. The gospel songwriter William J. Kirkpatrick put it beautifully when he penned these lines:

> Jesus, my Savior, is all things to me,
> Oh, what a wonderful Savior is He;
> Guiding protecting, o'er life's rolling sea,
> Mighty Deliverer—Jesus for me.
>
> Jesus in sickness, Jesus in health,
> Jesus in poverty, comfort, or wealth,
> Sunshine or tempest, whatever it be,
> He is my safety—Jesus for me.
>
> Jesus in sorrow, in joy, or in pain,
> Jesus my Treasure in loss or in gain,
> Constant Companion, where'er I may be,
> Living or dying—Jesus for me!

Jesus *is Jehovah-Shamah,* the LORD who is there when we need Him most. He is like an invisible Companion who tries to gain your attention and prove that He is "for you." But you must accept Him and acknowledge Him.

193

X NO He is NOT WITHIN EVERY ONE OF US humans ONLY those who have been regenerated. (Reborn)

The Lord Is There in Persecution

I have often been persecuted because of my ministry. When I was a missionary in Tibet, the Buddhist officials tried to drive me out of the country. When I was a pastor in the Philippines, the witch doctors tried to ban me from their villages. Even as a pastor in South Bend, I am sometimes persecuted. Politicians don't always like the stand I take on contemporary issues, and they try to silence me. Businessmen have tried to take control of the LeSEA ministry. I have been pressured and threatened. But, praise God, I have always known that the Lord would help me through all of those troubles.

Jesus warned His disciples:

There is no man that hath left house, or brethren, or sisters, or father, or mother, or wife, or children, or lands, for my sake, and the gospel's, but he shall receive an hundredfold now in this time, houses, and brethren, and sisters, and mothers, and children, and lands, with persecutions; and in the world to come eternal life. (Mark 10:29–30)

You see, Jesus wanted them to know what they could expect: a house (He will always provide shelter somewhere); brothers, sisters, mothers, and children (spiritually speaking); lands (when and if they are needed); *"with persecutions."* We Christians will have great privileges, yes; but we will endure persecution along the way. We should expect persecution. And we should know that the Lord is with us, even in the time of persecution.

If you're a Christian, you need to develop such a close relationship with the Lord that you'll be ready for persecution. You need to *digest* the Word of God so that you'll know what to do when you are persecuted. You need to be so fortified with God's Word and Spirit that you'll be able to thrive when persecution comes. You need to be ready to say, "This will drive me closer to the Lord. This will make me more mature in the Lord. Thank You for this trouble, Lord, because I know You mean it for my good."

> You must be fortified with God's Word and Spirit so you'll thrive when persecution comes.

As I mentioned in an earlier chapter, when I was a boy, Christian families decorated their homes with Scripture mottoes. You don't see many of them these days. They were often made out of painted cardboard with velvet letters. I remember sitting around our dinner table and seeing Mother point to a motto on the wall that said, "Christ is the Head of this house; the unseen Guest at every meal; the silent Listener to every conversation." That simple motto reminded us that the Lord was there, living with us, no matter how hard the going might get. (And believe me, the going got pretty tough during the Great Depression!)

I have often said on my television program that if you are what God wants you to be, and if you're doing what God wants you to do, when the devil calls on you he'll just get a busy signal! But if you're idle, or if you're doing something that is not ordained by the Lord, the devil gets an "open line" to talk with you.

Friend, let the motto over your home be *Jehovah-Shamah,* "the LORD is there." Keep well occupied with the work of the Lord by reading His Word and devoting yourself to prayer. If you'll do that, the Lord will make you the person that you should be in His sight.

MY PRAYER FOR YOU

O Lord, we know that everything in our lives will work out for Your glory if You are in them. We're so glad that You are the Lord who is always present in our lives. And we pray that we would acknowledge Your presence more fully by the way we live.

Lord, I thank You for the unsaved person who may be reading these words. I pray that You will convict this person of his or her sins and make him or her realize how desperate is the need to exalt You as the Lord of life. Forgive that sinner and take control of that heart right now.

And Lord, I thank You for the halfhearted Christian who may be reading these lines. May that person yearn to be Yours completely. Let him or her surrender all the things that have been held back from You, and let him or her turn the controls of that life over to You. Fill that one with Your Holy Spirit so that the world can look at that life and say, "Jehovah-Shamah, the Lord is there." And for that we will give You the praise.

Remember, the Lord of Hosts is there to fight your battles for you!

Fini
6 aug 2011
NOT all that
but skimpy

"What Must I Do to Be Saved?"

The apostle Paul and his missionary partner, Silas, were imprisoned at Philippi for preaching about Jesus. While in prison, they prayed and sang praises to God *"and the prisoners heard them"* (Acts 16:25). They were witnesses for the Lord, even in prison. While they were singing and praying, an angel of the Lord shook the prison with a strong earthquake. The keeper of the prison woke up, thinking all the prisoners must have escaped. So he drew his sword to commit suicide. But Paul cried, *"Do thyself no harm: for we are all here"* (Acts 16:28).

The prisonkeeper got a torch and ran into their prison cell, falling at their feet with fear. He cried, *"Sirs, what must I do to be saved?"* (Acts 16:30).

That has been the question of humanity since the very beginning of time: *What must I do to be saved from my sin? What must I do to be delivered from the fear and heartache that I have?* Paul and Silas were ready to answer the prisonkeeper. They said, *"Believe on the Lord Jesus Christ, and thou shalt be saved, and thy house"* (verse 31).

Now if Jesus was just another religious teacher, this advice would have been useless. The world has known plenty of religious teachers, but none of them have been able to save people from sin, fear, heartache, and death. Can you imagine how silly Paul and Silas would have sounded if they had said, "Believe on Socrates, and thou shalt be saved"? What if they had said, "Believe on Buddha, and thou shalt be saved"? Why, that would be ridiculous! No amount of religious teaching can save a person from sin.

But Paul and Silas said, *"Believe on the Lord Jesus Christ, and thou shalt be saved."* The apostle Peter said, *"Neither is there salvation in any other: for there is none other name under heaven given among men, whereby we must be saved"* (Acts 4:12). The apostle John said, *"Your sins are forgiven you for his name's sake"* (1 John 2:12).

The name of Jesus is powerful because Jesus Himself is powerful. Only He can save us from our sins, because He is God in the flesh. All the names of God that we have studied in this book apply to Jesus, because He is God. He is righteous; He is almighty; He is conqueror; He is healer. Every one of those attributes is true of Jesus Christ, because He is God Himself.

Perhaps you are asking the question that the Philippian jailer asked. Perhaps the burdens of your life are more than you can bear. You may be asking, "How can I be saved from the mess I'm in? How can I be delivered from the heartache of living like I do?"

If so, I have good news for you! It's the same good news that Paul and Silas gave the jailer: Believe on the Lord Jesus Christ, and you will be saved. Your whole family can be saved if all of you will turn your lives over to Him.

STEPS TO SALVATION

Here are some simple steps that you can follow to accept the Lord Jesus Christ right where you are:

1. *Repent of your sins.* The word *repent* means "to turn away from." When John the Baptist introduced Jesus to the people of his day, he said, *"Turn away from your sins... because the Kingdom of heaven is near!"* (Matthew 3:2 TEV). Peter said, *"Each of you must turn away from his sins and be baptized in the name of Jesus Christ, so that your sins will be forgiven"* (Acts 2:38 TEV). That's your first step to being saved. Admit that you have been sinning against God, and decide that you want to turn away from that sinful way of life.

2. *Confess that Jesus is your Savior.* In other words, admit that Jesus is the only One who can save you from your sins. He died on the cross of Calvary so you would not have to die in sin. You cannot earn your way into heaven by trying to do good; you can only trust Him to save you with His sacrificial blood. You need to confess that fact to Him, and confess it to your friends. The Bible says, *"That if thou shalt confess with thy mouth the Lord Jesus, and*

shalt believe in thine heart that God hath raised him from the dead, thou shalt be saved" (Romans 10:9).

3. *Believe that God will give you eternal life because you have placed your trust in Jesus.* This involves more than just accepting with your mind what the Bible says about Jesus. It means accepting God's promise with your whole heart, mind, and strength. Satan will try to make you doubt God's promise, but God never goes back on His Word. *"And this is the promise that he hath promised us, even eternal life"* (1 John 2:25).

You can take these steps right now, wherever you are. Salvation must be settled between you and God, and you can do that without anyone else helping you. But if you have trouble getting started with your prayer to Him, you might try this simple prayer:

Lord, I know that I am a sinner. I'm not living as You want me to live, and I can never live that way in my own strength. But Lord, I want to put sin out of my life once and for all, and begin living for You. So please forgive me for what I've done.

I believe You can save me from my sins, because You died on the cross and rose again. I confess that Your precious blood can cleanse the sin from my life. Only You can make me the person I ought to be. So I surrender my life to You.

Thank You for listening to my prayer, Lord. And thank you so much for the eternal life You have given me through Your death and resurrection from the grave. I give You all the praise for what You are going to do in my new life. I believe Your Word when it says I am "a new creature" now. I believe all the old things have passed away, and I am now completely different [2 Corinthians 5:17]. *Thank You for making me new, Lord. Amen.*

I hope that is your prayer today. I am praying that this study will cause you to accept Jesus as your Savior if you haven't already. When you do, you will praise Him along with the hymn writer Edward Perronet who said:

All hail the power of Jesus' name!

Let angels prostrate fall;

Bring forth the royal diadem,

And crown Him Lord of all!

ABOUT THE AUTHOR

L ester Sumrall (1913–1996), world-renowned pastor and evangelist, entered full-time service for God after experiencing what he recalls as the most dramatic and significant thing that ever happened to him.

At the age of seventeen as he lay on a deathbed, suffering from tuberculosis, he received a vision: Suspended in midair to the right of his bed was a casket; on his left was a large open Bible. He heard these words: "Lester, which of these will you choose tonight?" He made his decision: He would preach the Gospel as long as he lived. When he awoke the next morning, he was completely healed.

Dr. Sumrall ministered for over fifty-five years in more than 110 countries of the world, including Soviet Siberia, Russia, Tibet, and China.

He established Feed the Hungry in 1987. In addition, he wrote over 130 books. His evangelistic association (LeSEA), headquartered in South Bend, Indiana, is still actively spreading God's Word. Dr. Sumrall's goal was to win 1,000,000 souls for the kingdom of God, and the ministry continues this vision. LeSEA ministry includes such outreaches as the World Harvest Bible College, a teaching tape ministry, and numerous publications. Sumrall also founded LeSea Broadcasting, which owns and operates Christian television stations, a local radio station, and an international shortwave radio station, with the special purpose of bringing millions of souls to heaven.

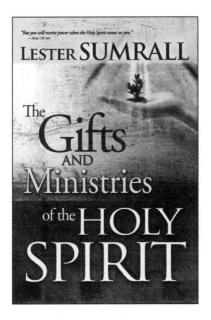

The Gifts and Ministries of the Holy Spirit
Lester Sumrall

The power of the Holy Spirit is available to you!
The gifts of the Spirit can destroy any force the devil might
use against Christians. You are a candidate for the gifts
of revelation, power, and inspiration. They will function
anywhere—right where you are now!

Dr. Lester Sumrall discusses subjects including
the charismatic renewal, the weapons of our warfare,
how you can receive the gifts, the devil's counterfeit,
and the purpose of ministry gifts. You can be included
in the great outpouring of God's Spirit!

ISBN: 978-0-88368-652-2 • Trade • 272 pages

WHITAKER
HOUSE
www.whitakerhouse.com

* I don't see this 9 ift listed in the
Scriptures

Pabulum

The Believer's Handbook
Lester Sumrall

World-renowned pastor and evangelist Lester Sumrall
offers straightforward answers to many of the burning
questions of life, including "Who is God, and does He
really care how I live my life?" He gives examples of his
encounters with angels, demons, and the living God that will
convince you there's more to this world than what you
can experience through your senses. Discover God's
perfect plan for earthly matters, too—supernatural
guidance on how to live your day-to-day life.
Are you ready for God to be revealed to you?

ISBN: 978-0-88368-852-6 • Trade • 624 pages

WHITAKER
HOUSE
www.whitakerhouse.com